Contributions to Management Science

For further volumes:
http.//www.springer.com/series/1505

Ingo Winkler

Contemporary Leadership Theories

Enhancing the Understanding of the
Complexity, Subjectivity and
Dynamic of Leadership

Physica-Verlag

Dr. Ingo Winkler
University of Southern Denmark
Dept. Border Region Studies
Alsion 2, A2
6400 Sønderborg
Denmark
inw@sam.sdu.dk

ISBN 978-3-7908-2157-4   e-ISBN 978-3-7908-2158-1
DOI 10.1007/978-3-7908-2158-1
Springer Heidelberg Dordrecht London New York

Library of Congress Control Number: 2009934501

Cover design: SPi Publisher Services

Printed on acid-free paper

Physica-Verlag is a brand of Springer-Verlag Berlin Heidelberg
Springer-Verlag is part of Springer Science+Business Media (www.springer.com)

Preface

As is the case with most books, this book also took some time to evolve. With the first ideas about writing it beginning in 2004, it was a rather long and busy process. However, it was also a process full of acquiring new knowledge, discussing topics with interesting people, gaining personal insights, and finally resulting in personal development. Particularly, I would like to thank Rainhart Lang, who contributed to my understanding of leadership and theory by providing many suggestions and a lot of advice. Furthermore, I would like to thank the students at Chemnitz University of Technology who patiently took part in my courses on contemporary leadership theory. From them I learned how newcomers to the subject understand what I have written in selected chapters and what should be consequently amended. Additionally, Elisabeth Schumann and Julia Heiber did a great job with proofreading the book and advancing the level of language. As English is not my first language it was sometimes necessary to remind me that expressing something in English is rather different from telling it in German. Finally, I am also grateful to the people at Springer, who helped me publishing this book.

Contents

Chapter 1
Aims and Outline of the Book

The aim of the book is to provide an overview of the basic theories and theoretical approaches of today's leadership research. The theories described in this book enhance the traditional thinking of traits and styles. At the same time, they supplement theoretical approaches found in top leadership journals nowadays, but also offer alternative explanations, and sometimes challenge mainstream leadership research. As a consequence, the book intends to highlight the diversity of theoretical approaches in contemporary leadership research. It focuses on approaches which can be regarded as well elaborated in terms of their clear theoretical contribution and the amount of existing research for each approach. Moreover, these theories and their ideas could be considered as central to present leadership research.

Leadership is often understood and used following a normative understanding, i.e., providing advice for effective leadership, resulting in followers' high performance and satisfaction. The key question examined by many researchers is: "What makes an effective leader?" (Van Seters and Field 1990, p. 29). In this regard, theoretical approaches to leadership are often related to leadership practice by incorporating normative statements into the theory itself. This book, however, takes a somewhat different perspective, namely that of emphasizing the descriptive and explicative content of contemporary theoretical approaches to leadership. Even if leadership research could be considered as dominantly normative, theories in this field, in my opinion, primarily serve to describe and explain leadership. This particular focus of the book, however, does not neglect any normative content included in some of the presented theories.

As written by a German scholar, the book develops a specific perspective on leadership theory that differs to some extent from the Anglo-Saxon's point of view. Differences can be particularly exemplified with the selection of theories considered as relevant but also with the presentation of each theoretical approach that represents a specific reading.

The selection of theories for this book was made considering two respects. Firstly, by applying a set of distinct attributes of current theoretical leadership approaches it was possible to differentiate between more recent and more classical

I. Winkler, *Contemporary Leadership Theories*, Contributions to Management Science, DOI 10.1007/978-3-7908-2158-1_1, © Springer-Verlag Berlin Heidelberg 2010

theories. These characteristics will be outlined in the next chapter. Secondly, relevant textbooks, scholarly books and encyclopedias on leadership (to mention just a few Bryman 1986; Hunt et al. 1987; Bass 1990a; Chemers and Ayman 1993; Yukl, 1994, 2001, 2006; Grint 1997; Northouse 1997, 2004, 2007; Goethals et al. 2004) as well as leading academic journals (e.g., The Leadership Quarterly, Leadership, The International Journal of Leadership Studies, Academy of Management Review, Administrative Science Quarterly) have been analyzed in order to disclose the most important developments of relevant approaches.

I also added the work of a German author, Oswald Neuberger, who has worked in the field of leadership for a long time and published several textbooks summarizing existing empirical and theoretical leadership research (e.g., Neuberger 1995, 2002). Moreover, he substantially contributed to the present German understanding of the micro-politics approach to leadership theory (e.g., Neuberger 1999) and the so-called symbolic leadership approach (e.g., Neuberger 1990). To provide a German perspective on leadership theory also means to include these theories in the book.

Nevertheless, the selection of approaches described in this book remains a subjective one. In the end, it was also my individual interpretation that led to the decision whether to include a particular theoretical approach in the book or not. This decision, however, was also the result of a subjective sense-making process. That means some scholars might see additional approaches that should be recognized (e.g., authentic leadership, shared leadership, complexity leadership theory) while others might claim that the book covers some dispensable conceptions. Being aware of that situation, I most welcome suggestions for further theories to be included and/or excluded in subsequent revisions of the book.

Turning to the content of the book, the first two theoretical approaches presented, i.e., the attribution theory of leadership and the psychodynamic approach to leadership, could be regarded as basic theoretical concepts of contemporary leadership research. Although both approaches are independent theories, they provide fundamental ideas widely used within current leadership research. For example, following the basic idea of the attribution theory of leadership, nearly all of the contemporary approaches define leadership as being ascribed by followers but not as an objective fact based on traits and behavior. In contrast, the psychodynamic leadership approach is based on deeply rooted understandings of leadership experienced and learned in early socialization which guide leader behavior and follower reaction, and lead to an emotional relation between leader and follower.

Following the description of the two basic theoretical approaches, the neo-charismatic leadership theory and the leader–member exchange theory are specified. Both approaches could be considered to be the most influential and most widely discussed theories nowadays, especially when having a look at top academic leadership journals. The ideas provided by scholars following these approaches constitute the main stream of leadership research today.

Subsequently, the idiosyncrasy credit model of leadership as theoretical approach is outlined. This approach follows the same ideas of the social exchange theory (e.g., Blau 1964; Homans 1958) as the leader–member exchange theory, but emphasizes different aspects, such as leader emergence. Overall, this model falls in the currently non-prominent but increasing body of research that focuses not only on the leader but also on followers and their role in the leadership relation (Marion and Uhl-Bien 2001).

The remaining four chapters deal with theoretical approaches whose ideas have been common in leadership research for quite a long time. However, aspects like sense-making and symbols covered by the symbolic leadership approach, as well as different interests and political behavior addressed by the micro-politics approach to leadership, but also roles and inter-role relations focused on by the role theory of leadership, and motivation and learning highlighted by the social learning theory of leadership are seldom fully recognized in the present work on leadership theory. To summarize, these perspectives offer fruitful insight into the theoretical understanding of leadership and provide a rich background for leadership research going beyond the mainstream.

Each chapter provides the main ideas of the approach referring to the most relevant scholars for each theory. Often, a leadership theory undergoes a development from its original ideas to aspects addressed in contemporary research. Where relevant, such developments are highlighted. At the end of each chapter, a short, yet not complete, description of basic pros and cons is presented. These selected strengths and shortcomings should assist readers' evaluation of the theory and provide issues to keep in mind when working with the approach.

Chapter 2
Characteristics of Contemporary Theoretical Approaches in Leadership Research

The focus on more recent theories more or less necessarily means to neglect classical leadership approaches, such as the trait approach, the behavior or style approach, and the situational leadership approach. These theories are criticized for their determined and narrow perspective, which fails to cover leadership reality. Classical approaches assume that there is a unidirectional personal influence of the leader on the followers. Leaders are traditionally seen as having a particular personality with traits different from those of followers. They are conceptualized as active players in the process of leadership. In contrast, followers are regarded as passive and reactive. Additionally, leadership relations in the context of a formal hierarchy are usually understood as situations that are socially predetermined. That means it is always clearly defined who is the supervisor/leader and who is the follower and, consequently, who has power and who does not. A last point of criticism addresses the lack of empirical evidence (e.g., Bryman 1996, 1999; Heller 2002). For example, classical leadership research failed to provide clear empirical evidence for the influence of traits on the emergence of leadership or leadership effectiveness as the result of a certain type of behavior. Following these critical reflections it becomes obvious that it is not sufficient to explain leadership by just concentrating on individual characteristics or patterns of leader behavior that might vary with situational differences. According to a statement expressed by Chemers (1997) some 10 years ago, it can be summarized that 50 years of leadership research have shown that simple answers, which emphasize the universal validity of characteristics, behaviors, or styles, are not suitable for explaining the dynamics of the leadership process (see also Yukl 1994, 2006).

However, the question arises as to what marks the contemporary approaches in order to explain leadership more appropriately? To answer this question, the following characteristics can be offered:

1. The majority of contemporary approaches conceptualize the process of leadership as a process of interaction. In classical theories there is a dominant reference to the characteristics and behavior of the leader (e.g., Rost 1991; Avolio 2005). In contrast, current approaches focus on leadership as a complex,

interactive process (e.g., Van Seters and Field 1990; Yukl 2006; Hollander 2008). Furthermore, recent approaches do not presume the existence of a pre-determined situation, in which leader and follower roles are clearly distributed according to the formal organizational structure. Instead, members of organizations, whatever their formal position, are usually seen as consciously acting individuals who are pursuing particular aims on the basis of their own and common interests and who are influencing each other mutually. Consequently, all members of an organization are capable of being leaders so that a clear distinction between leaders and followers on a formal basis is not possible. "Thus, leadership, like other categories that are used to classify people, may be a 'fuzzy category'" (Lord et al. 1982, p. 109).

2. In almost all contemporary leadership theories the significance of the subjective perception of the individual for developing and forming leadership relations is emphasized. Members of a group or an organization do not act based on an "objective reality," in which only economic performance is important. Instead, behavior is guided by their own subjective construction of reality which is shaped by past experiences as well as by current perceptions and expectations (e.g., Avolio 2005; Kezar et al. 2006). As a consequence, leadership reality is understood as being construed with perceptions and attributions playing a major part (Hunt 1984).

3. Contemporary approaches also draw a different picture of the leadership context, which is regarded as complex, dynamic, and ambiguous. Hence, diversity and complexity as well as a strong interconnectedness of environmental factors (instead of simple causalities), and the emphasis on change play an important role. Leadership is "a sequence of multidirectional, reciprocal influence processes among many individuals at different levels, in different subunits, and within executive teams" (Yukl 1994, p. 459). Leadership is conceptualized as a product of complex social relationships (Dachler 1988). Leadership cannot be seen irrespective of the logic and dynamic of the social system in which it is embedded because "changes in organizations over time, require a multifaceted explanation in which personal leadership will remain a constituent in a much broader concept" (Heller 2002, p. 399).

4. Current theoretical approaches on leadership emphasize to a greater extent the role of leadership research concerning describing and understanding in contrast to (premature) recommendations for effective leader behavior and normative models. They focus more on explaining leadership processes, describing typical leader behavior, and presenting why given behaviors occur in certain contexts (Yukl 2006). If behavioral recommendations are given, then this is usually done more carefully, less generalizing, and rarely out of a philosophy that anything is possible (see, for example, the practical implications provided by Kezar et al. 2006). Moreover, current leadership theories are accepting the limits of leader influence.

The majority of the contemporary theoretical concepts follow the implicit assumption that leadership has to be understood and researched by considering these aspects. Following Hunt's classification of different leadership approaches on a continuum from "objectivistic" to "subjectivistic" (Hunt 1991), they are more likely to be assigned to the subjectivistic perspective, as they tend to conceptualize reality as a field of symbolic discourse, as social construction, or as projection of human imagination. Even if traditional patterns of explanation are partially included in the argumentation of newer approaches, contemporary theories generally have to be understood as an advantage of the classical theories. The selection of the approaches discussed in this book resulted particularly from the fact that they have the above-mentioned characteristics in common. They, hence, come off a rigid and restricted understanding of organizations and hierarchies and, consequently, predetermined leadership contexts. Leadership is rather understood as a result of the various interactions between members of a given group, which is hardly ever predictable.

Chapter 3
Attribution Theory in Leadership Research

Introduction and Background

Attribution theory is basically dealing with the formation of individual opinions about the reasons of particular events or observations. This also includes opinions about the behavior of other people and about oneself. Attribution theory is usually seen as originating from the work of Heider (1958), Jones and Davis (1965) as well as Kelley (1967, 1972, 1973). It is argued that ordinary people use methods of ascribing reasons to observed events that are similar to the inductive approach used in scientific research. They try to identify the reasons for observed incidents and actions by collecting information which might be helpful for explaining them. More generally, in our everyday life we are constantly trying to form chains of cause and effect that link observed incidents (e.g., a traffic accident or a nervous breakdown of a colleague) and experiences (e.g., failing an exam) to possible reasons. Consequently, attributions are understood to play a crucial role in human categorization processes and, thus, in the reduction of ambiguity. By attributing causes to effects, observed or experienced incidents are linked to certain stimulus categories of the world in our mind. Hence, attributions provide order and increase the ability of a person to understand his/her own behavior and that of others. By linking incidents and actions to concrete reasons, they are interpreted and arranged by the observer. Based on this fact, the individual is then able to determine his/her own behavior.

The ideas of attribution theory are used in two regards within the field of leadership. Firstly, it is focused on the attribution of leadership qualities, which members of a group ascribe to an individual with regard to observed behavior (e.g., Calder 1977; Lord et al. 1984; Lord and Maher 1993). Secondly, it is concentrated on the superior's attributions based on his/her observations of an inferior's behavior (e.g., Mitchell and Wood 1980; Mitchell et al. 1981). In the following sections these two directions of attribution theory in leadership research are described in more detail. Furthermore, the extension provided by Martinko and Gardner (1987) is presented. These authors build on the work of Green and Mitchell (1979) and propose an interactive model of the leader/member attribution process.

I. Winkler, *Contemporary Leadership Theories*, Contributions to Management Science,   9
DOI 10.1007/978-3-7908-2158-1_3, © Springer-Verlag Berlin Heidelberg 2010

Leadership as Attributed Quality

This approach to attribution theory in leadership research can be traced back to Calder (1977) and has been later supplemented and changed by the work of Lord and his colleagues (e.g., Lord et al. 1984). Referring to this approach, leadership is a construct in the mind of human beings that does not exist independently from followers, but only in their perception (Calder 1977). "In other words, a person is a leader (good or bad) because others say so" (McElroy 1982, p. 413).

Leadership cannot be observed directly. Individuals of a group take note of the behavior of other group members or deduce a particular behavior from observed effects. Based on this information they ascribe certain leadership abilities to other people. In his model, Calder explains the process of attribution and provides answers to why particular attributes are perceived as leadership qualities. The model consists of four stages (see Fig. 1).

Following the so-called naive psychology of Heider (1958), Calder assumes that leadership is an everyday concept featuring certain personal qualities which can be described using our common language. These qualities – or the so-called general pre-understanding of leadership – vary (a) from group to group (e.g., street gang vs. top management of a company) and (b) according to the situation (e.g., crisis vs. a company's stable economic situation). People usually have such preconceptions and these ideas affect the leadership attribution process.

In the *first stage* of the model, a member of the group observes the behavior of the other members. The behavior can be observed either directly or it can be deduced from observed effects. For example, if someone observes the increasing performance of a department, conclusions will be drawn about the behavior of the head of department without having observed his/her behavior directly. In this context, it is important to notice that behavior is never seen as a mere fact but is always related to possible consequences or results (Calder 1977). This means, for example, that the observed behavior of "making a suggestion" will always be evaluated according to the consequences this behavior could induce (e.g., usefulness of this suggestion).

In the *second stage* of the model, members of a group infer from observed behavior additional patterns of behavior (not directly observed). If, for example, someone is talking a lot, the possibility increases that this person gets ascribed leadership qualities. This happens because from the observed behavior "much talking" other possible patterns of behavior (e.g., "can convince," "knows a lot") might be deduced (Calder 1977).

Subsequently, observed behavior of an individual is analyzed to the effect of determining whether it is different from the behavior of other group members. If a trainer is behaving in exactly the same way as the players, he cannot be spotted as the leader (Neuberger 1995, 2002). According to Calder, this analysis follows Kelley's concept of differences (Kelley 1967). The observer examines whether the observed or deduced behavior is different from the behavior of other members of the group. A clear distinction, however, can only be made if clear differences in

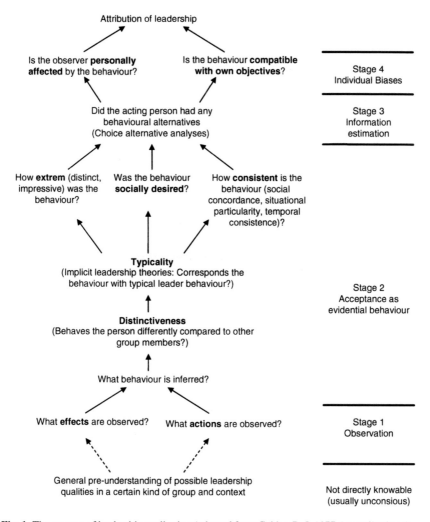

Fig. 1 The process of leadership attribution (adapted from Calder, B. J. 1977 An attribution theory of leadership, in: Staw, B. M./Salancik, G. R. (Eds.), New Directions in Organizational Behavior, St. Clair Press (Chicago), p. 196, with permission from the author)

the patterns of behavior in a group exist. If there are only minor differences in the behavior of the group members, the observer has difficulties detecting specific behavior the analysis should concentrate on. If major differences can be made out, however, single patterns of behavior can easily be taken as the basis for attribution.

The behavior which has been identified as variant is compared with the expectations the observer has concerning leadership behavior. This means behavior is compared with so-called implicit theories of leadership. Such everyday theories are part of implicit theories of organization (Meindl 1990) and have been developed in various processes of socialization. In particular, implicit theories of leadership are internalized concepts of typical leader qualities, typical leader behavior, and typical effects of leadership (e.g., Emrich 1999). Implicit leadership theories (ILTs) in a society can differ to a large extent and are, according to Calder, especially dependent on the social strata the follower belongs to and on previous observations of leader behavior. The observer interprets potential leadership behavior and behavioral effects which indicate leadership qualities on the basis of these implicit theories about leadership (Calder 1977). This means that people assume that observed behavior expresses particular characteristics of personality which, in relation to leadership, allow for conclusions about the existence of particular individual leadership qualities.

According to Calder, however, these conclusions are not sufficient for ascribing leadership qualities to certain individuals. Observers additionally analyze whether any alternative explanations exist in order to verify initial conclusions based on implicit theories. Here, Calder refers to the analysis of covariance proposed by Kelley (1973) in order to explain the process of assessment. The observer examines if observed behavior is persistent concerning temporal and situational aspects as well as if it is evaluated in the same way by others.

The following questions come up:

- If the conditions were similar and the task was the same, would other people behave in the same or different way? To what degree is the observed behavior associated with other individuals (*consensus*)?
- Is the deviant behavior of the observed person bound to the particular task or can this also be noticed in connection with other tasks? To what degree is the observed behavior associated with the same individual across different tasks (*distinctiveness*)?
- Is the observed behavior independent of time and situation or does it change with these variables? Is the observed behavior repeatedly associated with a particular individual over time (*consistency*)?

Depending on the answers to these questions, the follower ascribes the causes to the person or external factors, e.g., the task or temporal conditions. Table 1 outlines some examples of attributions as a result of covariance analysis.

Table 1 Attributions as a result of covariance analysis

Consensus (social concordance)	Distinctiveness (situational particularity)	Consistency (temporal consistency)	Attribution to
No, only the observed person behaves that way	No, the observed behavior is not bounded to the specific task	Yes, the observed behavior is independent of situation and time	Person (internal)
Yes, other people also behave in the same way	Yes, the observed behavior is bounded to the specific task	Yes, the observed behavior is independent of situation and time	Task (external)
Yes, other people also behave in the same way	No, the observed behavior is not bounded to the specific task	No, the observed behavior changes with situation and time	Time (external)

Moreover, it is analyzed in this stage whether the observed behavior was socially desired. According to Kelley (1967), the internal attribution referring to individual characteristics is less the more the observed behavior was considered as socially desired. In contrast, if the observed person had to overcome a particular social resistance, this would result in an internal attribution. Furthermore, it is analyzed whether the behavior was extreme enough (showing a significant difference in comparison to normal behavior).

In the *third stage* of the model, the observer analyzes whether the acting person would have had any behavioral alternatives. It is examined whether any other action of the possible leader (e.g., doing nothing) would have resulted in the same consequences. The more obvious the effects that can be traced back to the observed behavior, the more leadership is ascribed to the observed person. According to Calder (1977), extreme behavior may result in a weakened or no form of analysis of alternative modes of behavior.

In the *fourth stage* of the model, the attention is turned to the interests of the follower. Observed behavior and its evaluation are contrasted with his/her own objectives. The follower is testing to what extent he/she is influenced by the behavior of the leader and how much this behavior is affecting his/her own objectives. According to Calder (1977), followers are more likely to ascribe leadership qualities to a particular person based on observed behavior, the more it will serve their own personal interests.

In comparison to the classical trait theory of leadership, the process model of Calder points to the fact that leadership qualities cannot be generalized. Rather, they are context-specific ascriptions based on perceptions and interpretations of the members of a group. Leadership is a construct, which followers have developed in their minds. Furthermore, leadership is an attributed causal explanation. Following Kelley (1971) it has to be noted, however, that people tend to attribute causes to controllable factors. Consequently, the attribution of leadership derives partially from the wish to believe in the effectiveness and importance of individual action, as this is perceived as being more controllable than contextual factors (Pfeffer 1977). That means observed behavioral effects seem to be more often attributed to individuals (the leader) than to environmental or situational factors. Meindl et al. (1985) name this tendency the romance of leadership. They argue that people commonly believe that leaders are directly responsible for good and bad organizational outcomes. Hence, members of an organization follow the assumption that leaders are able to control the organization, regardless of other situational influences (Bligh and Schyns 2007). Referring to this effect, Bass (1995) questions whether effects in organizations are ascribed to leadership with respect to superiors while they are actually caused by other organizational and/or environmental factors.

As outlined, the model of Calder has been further developed by the works of Lord and his colleagues (e.g., Lord and Maher 1990; Lord and Smith 1983). While Calder's model describes an all-embracing rational process of information processing with ILTs being only a part of it, Lord is convinced that people are more often classified as leaders due to a more unconscious process of comparison with ILTs playing the major part. It is recognized that people engage in rational information processing; however, such a process only occurs with important or surprising events (Martinko et al. 2007). More typically, the behavior of an observed person is compared with so-called leadership prototypes as part of ILTs (Lord et al. 1984). Lord and Foti (1986, p. 25) define a prototype as an "abstract set of features commonly associated with the members of a category." A leadership prototype is therefore seen as an abstraction of the most representative features (characteristics and behaviors) of a person belonging to the category "leader." On the basis of criteria such as behavior, appearance, clothing, and situational factors, observed behavioral patterns are matched with internalized typical characteristics of a leader and leadership (Lord and Maher 1990). Internalized means that leadership prototypes are embedded in knowledge structures developed through general experiences as well as through experiences in particular organizational settings (Lord and Maher 1993). In short, "the decision to label an individual as a leader depends on the extent to which the features of a target overlap with the features that distinguish the leader category or prototype" (Brown et al. 2004, p. 138).

Today, empirical research on the attribution of leadership to certain persons usually follows the concept of ILTs. The early concept of Calder is rarely mentioned in current research. ILTs may be defined as learned cognitive categories that enable a person to differentiate between leadership and non-leadership and, thus, to classify others as leaders (Fischbein and Lord 2004). To the extent that a person matches one's preconception of a leader's personal traits, abilities, and behaviors, he/she is considered a leader (Hoyt 2008). Leadership is understood as an emerging social process produced by the interaction of a variety of factors, including context, tasks, group histories, and personal qualities of leaders and followers (Yukl 2006).

Leadership attribution is understood as being formed by recognition-based processes of leadership perception or inference-based processes of leadership perception. The former involves an automatic comparison of the features exhibited by a stimulus type of a perceiver's prototype or ILT. If a sufficient match occurs between the observed person (the potential leader) and a leadership prototype, then the observed person is likely to be seen as a leader (Fischbein and Lord 2004). In other words: Leadership is recognized from the behaviors and qualities revealed in interaction (Lord and Maher 1993). Within the latter process leadership is attributed to an individual based on knowledge of his/her performance. Lord and Maher put it as follows: "(People) assume that a major function of leaders is to produce good performance outcomes, and they infer leadership from knowledge of successful task or organizational performance" (Lord and Maher 1993, p. 55). Subsequently, observers may infer effective leadership based on knowledge of good performance. In contrast, knowledge of poor performance may tend to lower leadership perceptions. According to Fischbein and Lord (2004), the two types of leadership processes can act together. Hence, ILTs involve both the knowledge on leadership categories and the functional relation between category attributes to, for example, performance outcomes (Medvedeff and Lord 2006).

Starting from the initial investigation by Eden and Leviatan (1975) today we face numerous empirical studies on ILTs. Empirical ILT research among others has concentrated on the content of implicit leadership theories, on the processes of information processing, on the influences of the context on ILTs, and on the effects on leaders and followers. It is impossible to refer to all these aspects in this chapter; however, a few research topics should be addressed, namely contents of ILTs, contextual influences on ILTs, and effects of ILTs on leaders and followers.

An important role among studies that focus on contents of ILTs plays the empirical work of Offermann et al. (1994), which could be labeled as fundamental. They elaborated eight dimensions of ILT content, i.e., sensitivity, engagement, despotism, charisma, attractiveness, masculinity, intelligence, and strength, with altogether 41 behaviors and traits. In the same year, Kenney et al. (1994) studied newly imposed leaders without previous experiences with their group. They found that such leaders could be described with 16 leadership dimensions that differ in some aspects from Offermann et al.'s categorization. The work of Offermann et al. (1994), however, served as a basis for nearly all further studies on ILT content.

Studies on effects of ILTs usually address the question of how knowledge about preferred leadership behavior of followers and the perceived quality of the leader–member relationship also explains subsequent behavior of followers (e.g., Engle and Lord 1997; Epitropaki and Martin 2005). For example, Kraus and Gemmill (1990) in their study found that followers attribute more responsibility for success-ful task fulfillment to leaders if the observed behavior corresponds with the expected behavior based on followers' ILTs. Consequently, followers' leadership prototypes influence their favored leader characteristics and leadership styles.

Research on contextual influences on ILTs also addressed contents; however, they did not focus on the actual content of ILTs but highlighted differences in ILT content depending on various situational influences. Nearly all studies use a quan-titative methodology (Schyns and Meindl 2005) with large samples in order to achieve generalizations about situational differences in individual ILTs. Contextual influences addressed by empirical works are socialization (e.g., Keller 1999; Ayman-Nolley and Ayman 2005), societal culture (e.g., Den Hartog et al. 1999; Konrad 2000), organizational crises (e.g., Pillai 1996; Hunt et al. 1999), social distance between leader and followers (e.g., Shamir 1995; Yagil 1998), gender (e.g., Maher 1997; Müller and Schyns 2005), and follower's personality (e.g., Keller 1999; Felfe 2005).

Leader's Attributions Based on Observed Behavior

This approach to attribution theory in leadership research is concerned with the process of how leaders attribute causes to observed follower behavior and the subsequent leader reaction (e.g., Green and Mitchell 1979; Mitchell and Wood 1980; Mitchell et al. 1981). Attributions are understood as cognitions which influence the leader's behavior toward the followers. The "attribution phase," i.e., perception and active information processing by the superior, is considered to be only one phase of a two-stage process. The particular behavior of the superior is also resulting from a second stage called "decision phase," following the information processing. In this phase the leader draws consequences from the causal attribution and chooses an appropriate behavior. Consequently, this approach understands leadership as a two-stage process: Firstly, there is the phase of diagnosis in which the superior is ascribing the causes for performance; and secondly, the decision phase includes the selection of an appropriate reaction from a range of alternatives. Figure 2 gives a summarized overview of this process.

It can be seen that the key steps of the model are (1) the observation of subordinate behavior, (2) the subsequent causal attribution by the superior, and (3) the evaluation of the appropriate leader behavior by the superior based on this attribution. In the following section the model is described in detail.

Stage of Diagnosis

Superiors make causal attributions based on their observation of subordinate behavior. They try to uncover the actual cause of the observed behavior by applying a covariance analysis (A). They aim at linking the observed behavior of the follower with the variable which is changing simultaneously. Following the covariance analysis of Kelley (1973), leaders can attribute the behavior of followers to three causes: the *personality* of the follower, the *task* and its degree of difficulty, and the *situational context* under which the follower is fulfilling the task (Green and

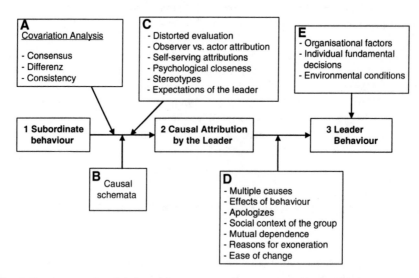

Fig. 2 Two-stage model of leader attribution and behaviour (adapted from Neuberger, O. (1995). Führen und Geführt werden [To lead and to be led]. Stuttgart: Ferdinand Enke, p. 204, with permission of Lucius & Lucius)

Table 2 Leader attributions as result of co-variance analysis

Consensus (social concordance)	Distinctiveness (situational context)	Consistency (temporal consistency)	Attribution to
Only the observed employee is making mistakes when doing this task	The observed employee is repeatedly making mistakes when doing the same task	The observed employee is always making mistakes, with other tasks also	Person (internal)
All employees are making mistakes when doing this task	The observed employee is only making a one-time mistake when doing this task	The observed employee is always making mistakes	Task (external)
All employees are making mistakes when doing this task	The observed employee is repeatedly making mistakes when doing the same task	The observed employee is normally not making any mistakes	Time (external)

Mitchell, 1979). The following questions are supposed to provide essential information (see, for example, Brown et al. 2004):

- If the conditions were similar and the task was the same, would other employees behave similarly or differently (*consensus*)?
- Is the observed behavior of the follower bound to the given situation or can it also be noticed in connection with other situations (*distinctiveness*)?
- Is the observed behavior exhibited in similar situations at different times (*consistency*)?

Depending on the answers of these questions the leader develops an assumption about the cause(s) of the observed follower behavior. These causes can be ascribed to the acting person (internal causes such as abilities, efforts, personality) or to the situational context (external causes such as difficulty of the task, number of available information). Table 2 provides an example of attributions as a result of the covariance analysis by the leader.

Having access to sufficient information the leader is able to comprehensively evaluate the follower's behavior by following the cognitive process described above. However, if information is insufficient, contradictory, or if the leader is short of time, simple standard interpretations come into operation. These so-called causal schemata (B), i.e., the assumption about how two or more causal factors interact in relation to a specific kind of effect (Kelley 1972), are used by the superior to draw conclusions about the causes of observed behavior. The scheme for classifying causal dimensions proposed by Weiner and colleagues is most commonly used in leadership literature (see Table 3).

According to this schema, the leader only takes two variables into account in order to evaluate the causes of observed behavior (McElroy and Hunger 1987). "Locus of control" is defined as the degree to which individuals ascribe success or failure to personal or situational aspects. "Stability" is defined as the degree to which the perceived causes of behavior are of relatively permanent or variable nature. Subsequently, success or failure can be attributed to ability, effort, task difficulty, or luck.

Table 3 Causal schemata

	Locus of control	
Stability	Internal (inside the person)	External (situational factor)
Stable	Ability	Task difficulty
Variable	Effort	Luck

Causal schemata (adapted from Weiner, B., Frieze, I., Kukla, A., Reed, L., Rest, S., Rosenbaum, R. M. (1987). Perceiving the causes of success and failure. In E. E. Jones, D. E. Kanouse, H. H. Kelley, R. E. Nisbett, S. Valins, B. Weiner, B. (Eds.), Attribution: Perceiving the causes of behavior (pp. 95-120). Hillsdale, NJ: Lawrence Erlbaum Associates, p. 96, with permission of Bernard Weiner)

Furthermore, a range of aspects concerning social perception (C) play a role as well during the evaluation of the employees' behavior by the leader (Green and Mitchell 1979; Mitchell et al. 1981; Hughes et al. 1996). The aspects described in the following list serve as moderators and can significantly influence the rational attribution process:

- *Misevaluation due to a sample that is not representative:* If the leader is inexperienced and, hence, has little knowledge about comparable situations or if the leader has insufficient information about the situation, observed behavior is probably misevaluated. As a consequence, the leader ascribes other causes to observed behavior than he/she would have done with sufficient information or a lot of experience on similar situations.
- *Actor–observer bias:* The superior, in this case the observer, is more likely to see the causes for poor performance in the person of the follower but not in situational aspects. In contrast, followers ascribe causes for their failure to external circumstances, e.g., the difficulty of the task. This tendency is labeled "actor–observer bias." According to Jones and Nisbett (1987, p. 80), "there is a pervasive tendency for actors to attribute their actions to situational require-ments, whereas observers tend to attribute the same actions to stable personal dispositions." That means individuals are explaining others' behavior by refer-ring to internal personal dispositions of the observed person while giving reasons for their own behavior based on the external situation.
- *Self-serving attributions:* Leaders, like all human beings, tend to maintain a positive self-image. They avoid attributions which would work against a partic-ular, i.e., positive, perception of their ego. As a consequence, poor performance of employees is not seen as the leader's failure but is attributed to external factors. In contrast, positive performance of employees is ascribed to the leader's own behavior.
- *Psychological closeness between leader and follower:* A social relationship that is strong and in which leader and follower know each other well influences the attribution made by the superior. In case of psychological closeness, the super-ior's attributions as observer become more similar to those of the follower. Subsequently, the leader follows the perceptions of the follower that the causes

of the follower's mistake are located in external aspects. In contrast, an increasing psychological distance between the leader and the follower will also increase the discrepancy between leader and follower attributions.

- *Stereotypical evaluation due to personal characteristics:* Stereotypes hold by the superior influence the perception and attribution. Particular patterns of behavior are associated with the mere affiliation of a follower to a certain group (e.g., in terms of gender, nationality, religion). So, holding, for example, gender stereotypes will influence the more rational process of attribution in a way that the observed behavior is linked to stereotyped personal characteristics and is thus ascribed to the person.
- Expectations of the leader: If employees are acting according to the leader's expectations, an internal attribution (e.g., ability or effort) will be the result. However, if the observed behavior deviates from expectations, an external attribution, such as task difficulty, will follow.

As a consequence, the phase of diagnosis should not be understood as pure rational ascription of causes to observed behavior. The cognitive process is rather influenced by various social aspects that affect perceptions and interpretations. It is crucial whether the superior is making an internal or external attribution. This attribution will provide the basis for the reactions considered in the subsequent decision-making process.

Stage of Decision

The second phase of the model describes the process of the superior's decision making about an appropriate reaction. Following the basic ideas of the attribution theory, internal attributions lead to personal reactions (e.g., punishment of the inferior), whereas external attributions result in interferences with the work environment (e.g., changing the difficulty of the task). Besides others, Ashkanasy (1989, 1995) was able to demonstrate that such a principal relationship between attributions and reactions exists (see Martinko et al. 2007 for an extensive review of empirical research on the Green and Mitchell model). However, as results of empirical studies disclosed a variance of reactions, it is not clear if this relationship is always valid. Moreover, it has to be questioned on what aspects the intensity of the reaction depends. Apparently, the reaction itself as well as the intensity of the reaction is influenced by the following effects (D):

- The ascription of *multiple causes* (individual and situational) to the observed behavior increases the insecurity of the superior regarding an appropriate reaction. Consequently, extreme sanctions are less likely to be imposed. Instead, the employee will be further tested in order to acquire more clarity on the exact causes of the observed behavior.
- The *effects of the observed behavior* will affect the intensity of the superior's reaction. Even if the causes for poor performance are attributed to the person of

the follower, the subsequent behavior of the leader varies according to the effect this behavior has had. The worse the consequences of a mistake are evaluated, the more severe will be the punishment.

– *Apologies* of the employee lead to fewer sanctions. If an employee apologizes for the mistake and is repentant, the reaction of the superior will be less severe.
– The *social context of the group* influences the reaction of the superior. Popular and acknowledged group members (e.g., an employee with high status) are punished less severely than, for example, underdogs.
– *Mutual dependence* between superior and subordinates has a considerable influence on the reaction of the superior. When recognizing a certain dependence on followers, the superior rather forms his/her reaction by looking at the situation from the follower's point of view.
– If the follower can provide *plausible reasons serving as proofs for exoneration*, negative reactions by the superior are weakened or neutralized. Hence, the follower is not punished at all or in a less severe way.
– Superiors are more likely to focus their reactions on changing the behavior of the person than on changing the situational context. This tendency is labeled *ease of change* and follows the general perception that the behavior of employees can be influenced more easily than changing structures or organizational regulations.

Drawing a conclusion from the above-mentioned influences, it becomes apparent that the decision-making process also is affected by several aspects of social perception and interaction. As Fig. 2 further demonstrates, the decision process is also shaped by general organizational aspects, individual fundamental decisions, and environmental conditions (E). For example, superiors will usually be committed to a particular behavior due to formal organizational structures and regulations, even if they were to act differently on account of their causal attribution. In sum, the behavior of superiors is not only an outcome of attributions of an observed behavior but is also influenced by a set of external aspects.

An Interactive Model of the Leader/Member Attribution Process

In 1987, Martinko and Gardner proposed an interactive attributional model. Extending the work of Mitchell and his colleagues they emphasized the interactive dyadic nature of the attributional process. Both leader and member take an active part in this process and their behavior is influenced by the interplay between their attributions and responses. Figure 3 outlines the basic ideas of the model.

As the model indicates, the proposed concept covers leader attributions and simultaneously member attributions and responses. Attributions made by the leader or member are moderated by attributional biases and individual difference variables. Particularly, the actor–observer bias, the self-serving bias, the false consensus effect, and hedonic relevance are highlighted as attributional biases. Individual difference variables are self-esteem or susceptibility, among others.

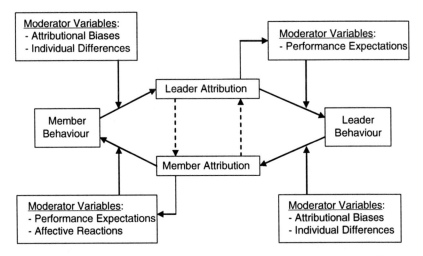

Fig. 3 Interactive attributional model of leader/member relations (adapted from Martinko, M. J., & Gardner, W. L. (1987). The leader/member attribution process. Academy of Management Review, 12(2), p. 237. Copyright 1987 by Academy of Management (NY). Reproduced with permission of Academy of Management (NY).)

Martinko and Gardner point out that leader and member make causal attributions using covariation analysis and/or causal schemata. Advancing earlier work of attribution theory of leadership they propose, however, that the communicated attributions result in "adjustments in the attributions of either or both parties" (Martinko and Gardner 1987, p. 236). For example, a leader's attribution of observed behavior to internal or external causes influences both his/her future performance expectations as well as the behavior toward the member. The member's response depends on the perception of the appropriateness of the leader's behavior and results in performance attributions (internal or external). Distinct member task directed behavior which is based on the member performance attributions is moderated by his/her (altered) performance expectations as well as affective reactions (Martinko and Gardner 1982). To close the circle, the specific member behavior is observed by the leader and forms the basis for subsequent attributions. As a consequence, both leader and member behaviors are in part shaped by the similarities and differences in their attributions for good and bad member performance (Martinko et al. 2007). It is hypothesized that leaders tend to attribute observed member failure to internal causes (e.g., member's ability or effort), whereas members tend to see the causes for failure in the external environment (e.g., task difficulty). These differences in the attributions also lead to differences in leader and member behavior, and thus to differences in the perceived appropriateness of the other party's behavior. Hence, conflicting attributions could result in tensions in the leader–member relation.

Selected Pros and Cons

A strong advantage of this approach (in particular referring to the work of Calder and Lord) is that incorporating ideas of attribution theory allows addressing the complex interplay between organizational and personal aspects with leadership emergence. The result that leadership is not just an objective quality or a character-istic of an individual but an external attribution has been adopted by most of the contemporary leadership theories nowadays. The evaluation of observed leadership behavior patterns and the consequences emerging from that are not simply a rational but a complicated process depending on social influences and sometimes "blurred" interpretations.

Additionally, the work by Mitchell and his colleagues shows that supervisors undergo an intensive cognitive process, which is also moderated by a set of social aspects when assessing observed behaviors of subordinates. Consequently, the superior's behavior also is based on his/her subjective attribution of causes and not on objective criteria.

One problematic fact of the attribution theory in leadership is the assumption that the process of forming attributions in principal is a rational one. For example, the influence of emotions and selective perceptions on cognitive processes of information processing is partly neglected. In this regard, Hughes et al. (1996) point to the fact that ILTs also work as a "perceptual set." Consequently, the behavior of particular persons or groups of people is perceived as more or less strong and is, therefore, available for cognitive processing in varying degrees (see also Feldman 1981).

In addition, social influences on the process of attribution are treated as moder-ating factors. It could be questioned, however, if these aspects of social perception and interaction in the end constitute the normal case of attribution and if the rational attribution process is considered just as fiction or as exception. Referring to the various moderators and constraints, Green and Mitchell (1979) raised concerns about the direct link between a leader's attributions and leader behavior.

A final point of criticism addresses different attributions of poor and good performances. In fact, almost all empirical studies focusing on superiors' behavior have analyzed situations of poor follower performances. However, these results are often not questioned but uncritically transferred to attributions of good performance (Shaver 1985).

Chapter 4
Psychodynamic Leadership Approach

Introduction and Background

According to Stech (2006), the basic ideas of the psychodynamic leadership approach can be summarized as follows. People gain their initial experiences with leadership from the day they are born. Parents function as first leaders within the family. Following the basic assumption of this approach, these early experiences of leadership form an unconscious basis for future behavior as leader and follower. Experiences of childhood and adolescence are mirrored in patriarchal, matriarchal, or familial leadership patterns and, therefore, are mainly responsible for the way members of organizations act as leaders or react to authority. Within socialization we also learn the unconscious archaic image of the powerful male, which is seen as a basic source for leadership (Goethals 2004). If a leader mirrors this image consisting of a strong and independent individual who imposes his will on other group members, then he is reawakening this archaic image, which leads to obedience in the group. The psychodynamic leadership approach follows the tradition of management research using the psychodynamic approach, with Zaleznik (1977) and Maccoby (1977) probably being the most important representatives.

Basic Concepts

The psychodynamic leadership approach can be traced back to ideas in Freud's psychoanalysis (e.g., Freud 1938) as well as to other representatives of depth psychology. Depth psychology basically deals with motives of human behavior in which the unconscious is regarded as an important factor for individual perception and behavior. Although authors of depth psychology have not dealt with personal and social dimensions of management in companies, the psychodynamic leadership approach makes use of their terms, hypotheses, and models. In particular, this

I. Winkler, *Contemporary Leadership Theories*, Contributions to Management Science, DOI 10.1007/978-3-7908-2158-1_4, © Springer-Verlag Berlin Heidelberg 2010

theoretical approach is based on the psychoanalytic concepts of "family of origin," "process of maturation or individualization," "dependence and independence," as well as of "regression," "suppression and shadow of the Ego" (see Stech 1997, 2004). Subsequently, the basic concepts are briefly outlined for a better understanding of the theory.

Family of Origin

This concept is the basis for understanding adult behavior, as almost every individual is brought up in a family. It is the role of the parents – as the first leaders in one's life – to socialize their children, particularly in early childhood. According to Kets de Vries (1997), the first three years of life are of particular importance, as during these years the core patterns of personality are shaped. Yet, the process of socialization – that is, teaching the child the institutionalized conventions of society – is not one-sided. By responding to the needs of a child, a mutual parent-child adaptation develops resulting in interdependency. As a consequence, experiences with leadership made in the process of socialization in early childhood include experiences as both follower and leader. These encounters with leadership within the family are decisive for future behavior as adults. Subsequently, it is possible to explain the behavior of executives and the reaction of subordinates based on experiences made in their childhood.

Process of Maturation and Individualization

As a child grows older, he/she becomes more and more independent from the parents. Becoming an adolescent and later on an adult is part of the process of maturation. Yet, due to early socialization, a person still carries inside him/her the parents' ideas about what is right and wrong in society, which influences his/her actions and thinking. For the psychodynamic leadership approach, the relationship between a child and persons of authority is a key element in the maturation process. The way the child, the adolescent, and later on the adult behave towards a person of authority (e.g., a leader) is to a great extent dependent on the degree of authority experienced in the relationship between the child and the parents. Although reactions are difficult to predict, an authoritarian relationship in early childhood could result in either obeying or defying behavior. The psychodynamic leadership approach assumes that the process of maturation (with respect to the process of individualization) modifies experiences made in the family of origin. Both concepts are regarded as important influences on the behavior of leaders and followers in companies.

Dependence and Independence

Employees in organizations face different behavior patterns of executives. How they react to more authoritarian or more participative leadership behavior depends on their experiences made in childhood and adolescence. From a psychodynamic perspective, an employee can react in three different modes towards the leader's behavior: in a dependent, defying or independent way. The first two patterns of behavior are self-explanatory. Responding in an independent way implies that the employee tests his/her room of maneuver of different behavior patterns in the leader–follower relationship. Furthermore, the subordinate questions the given instructions in terms of their meaning and rejects those which do not make sense to him/her. In addition, the mode of the leader's behavior is related to their childhood. Hence, an authoritarian or participative leadership style is regarded as rooted in an authoritarian or antiauthoritarian upbringing in childhood.

Regression

By carrying out behavioral training it is at least partially possible to influence the behavior of members of an organization. Especially executives are trained in various leadership seminars. The aim of such training is to learn how to cope with followers in different kinds of situations and, thus, to respond in an appropriate style of leadership behavior. However, in stressful or unusual situations it can be noticed that even trained leaders fall back into "old" patterns of behavior. This phenomenon is called regression and means the return to the basic patterns of behavior "learned" in childhood and adolescence. These deeply rooted patterns cannot be replaced by specific training but are just superimposed by it.

Suppression and Shadow of the Ego

Through the process of upbringing, with respect to socialization, thoughts and emotions which are deemed unacceptable by a society are deeply embedded in the consciousness of an individual. Patterns of behavior which refer to unaccepted thoughts and emotions will be suppressed and partially replaced by other modes of behavior. For example, in Western societies solving interpersonal conflicts by violent means is usually regarded as unacceptable behavior in most situations. Consequently, the child is taught to use different behavior patterns in order to solve such conflicts, e.g., by arguing. In the process of socialization the child and later on the adolescent learns to suppress unaccepted behavior in many situations and to adapt to behavioral norms of the society. A similar concept focuses on the often suppressed shadow of a person. In other words, if patterns of behavior that are usually regarded as undesired or negative are observed in one's own behavior, then one aims to suppress them. However, such suppression partially takes place only in a person's self-perception but not in his/her actual behavior. Consequently, other people continue to perceive these negative patterns. Although, for example, executives suppress certain authoritarian modes of behavior which they deem unacceptable, external perception by followers can draw a picture in which these patterns continue to turn up.

Identification and the Emergence of Leadership

The description of the basic psychological ideas demonstrates the close relationship between the psychodynamic leadership approach and the ideas of depth psychology. Regarding the emergence of leadership the psychodynamic leadership approach applies the concept of projective identification (e.g., Ogden 1979, 1986). In this context, however, projective identification is not understood as a defense mechanism, i.e., projecting unwanted feelings or beliefs into another person (Pervin 1993), but is rather defined as a mechanism in which a part of the self is projected onto an external object (Ogden 1979). In other words, projection is understood as a "psychological mechanism of transferring or assigning to another an idea or impulse that really belongs to oneself" (Kets de Vries 1989, p. 22). Leadership emerges when an individual represents the group member's ideal (Goethals 2004). In this case, the group member projects his/her self-ideal, i.e., the picture of the ideal self, onto an admired person (the potential leader), whereupon the potential follower emotionally identifies with this person (see Fig. 1).

The self-ideal, "what one wants to be," as substructure of the superego is given up and transferred to the admired person. Consequently, the idealized object/individual is used as orientation for acting and thinking instead of the self-ideal. In Fig. 1, individual B serves as an idol and is perceived as the person representing all characteristics and behavior patterns individual A regards as ideal. An emotional bond develops, or, in other words, the follower falls in love with the leader (Goethals 2004). A group of followers emerges when several followers replace their self-ideals with the idealized person of the leader (see Fig. 2).

If several members of a group project their self-ideal to the same admired person, then this individual is collectively recognized as the leader. "A group ego ideal comes into being" (Kets deVries 1988, p. 270) serving as a "new" self-ideal of all group members. Putting it differently, group members follow the leader as they perceive him/her as the idealized role model representing their self-ideal.

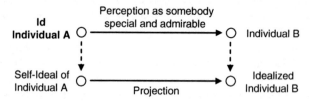

Fig. 1 Projection of the self-ideal

Fig. 2 Identification with the
leader by several followers

Person A

Identification

The idealization of the leader results in the fact that the leader is perceived positively while negative characteristics are denied. The affective relation to the leader produces a certain amount of freedom from criticism (Goethals 2004). Put simply, the leader as the chosen object of idealization is overvalued (see Cluley 2008 for a more basic explanation of this process). In turn, leadership is maintained by the mechanism of splitting. As a matter of principle, the leader is perceived positively while his/her negative characteristics are denied. Hence, leadership represented by the idealized person is always judged positively and, hence, is stabilized. Negative experiences and outcomes are attributed to the situation or task difficulty but not to the person of the leader. However, as soon as the leader fails to fulfill the group's needs of identification, his/her status as group leader will be deprived. As a consequence, group members start to attribute negative experiences to the leader. He/she is no longer admirable and loses his/her reputation. Then, the former leader is principally perceived as "evil" and, for example, is ascribed the role of the scapegoat for the perceived problems.

Analysis of Leadership Relations

Within the psychodynamic leadership approach relations between leaders and followers in organizations are often examined using transactional analysis (e.g., Berne 1961; Harris 1967). The aim of this method is to analyze verbal and nonverbal behavior in order to uncover the roles individuals occupy in the leader–follower relationship. Following Berne's ideas, it is assumed that personality consists of three so-called ego-states, i.e., a specific mixture of behavior, thoughts, and feelings. These ego-states are the child ego-state, the parent ego-state, and the adult ego-state.

–   The child ego-state expresses behavior, thoughts, and feelings that are similar to those in people's childhood. This ego-state is revealed in childlike behavior, guided by and expressing a lot of emotions.
–   The parent ego-state reflects parental behavior people experienced in their childhood. The behavior is often an imitation of the behavior observed with parents, in terms of their reaction to different situations.
–   The adult ego-state is associated with systematic and logical information processing. Decisions and predictions are made in a rational way absent of rather "disturbing" emotions.

Fig. 3 Ego states of leader
and subordinate (Stech, E. L.
(2006). Psychodynamic
approach. In P. G. Northouse
(Ed.), Leadership. Theory and
Practice. Thousand Oaks:
Sage, p. 242. Copyright 2006
by Sage Publications Inc
Books. Reproduced with
permission of Sage
Publications Inc.)

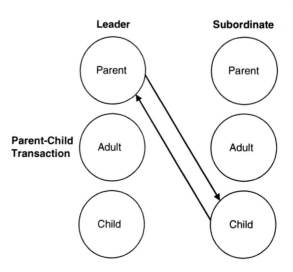

These ego-states are supposed to have universal value and each of us is operating in
one of these states (Mullins 2007). This means also that in the leader–follower
relation each party is acting as child, parent, or adult (see Fig. 3).

Turning to the relations, complementary and crossed reactions can be distinguished (Mullins 2007). Stable patterns of interaction in the leader–subordinate
relation emerge when the arrows representing the transactions are parallel (complementary reactions). In the case of Fig. 3, the leader acts in a parental state (e.g.,
as the father) and the employee reacts in the state of the child. From the followers'
point of view, former relationships with the parents are transferred to the current
relationship with the leader (Bryman 1992). Instable patterns in leader–subordinate
relationships occur when transactions between mismatching roles exist (crossed
reactions). For example, the leader behaves in the ego-state of the parent, whereas
the employee reacts not in the state of the child but as an adult.

Based on transaction analysis different types of leadership relations can be
identified which are explained with the concepts of depth psychology. Here, the
leader is usually assigned the parental state, bringing back to followers (that are
ascribed to the child state) the security and stability experienced in childhood (e.g.,
Kets de Vries 1989; Sankowsky 1995).

Types of Leaders

Based on the core concepts of the psychodynamic leadership approach several
authors proposed different types of leaders (e.g., Argyris 1957; Maccoby 1977;
Kets deVries and Miller 1984; Kets de Vries 1989). To provide an overview, the
two early typologies of Argyris (1957) and Maccoby (1977) as well as the later
classification of Maccoby (2000) are introduced.

Argyris (1957) distinguished between so-called mature (i.e., adult) and imma-ture (i.e., child) personalities. As with many classifications of types of leaders and followers, the psychodynamic leadership approach also assigns the role of the adult to the leader. Argyris critically points out that most organizations treat their staff as rather immature personalities. Thus, organizational structures, practices, and beha-viors are designed in a context that implicitly or explicitly ascribes the role of the child to the followers.

Maccoby (1977) provided an overview of manager types. Quoting numerous examples of leaders from the business and political sphere he introduced the following four types of managers:

- The down-to-earth and objective craftsman.
- The power-hungry jungle fighter who focuses on conflicts.
- The company man who is interested in the security of the company and cares for his subordinates.
- The gamesman who sees his tasks as a challenge and for whom competition itself offers an incentive.

Maccoby's evaluation showed that the gamesman seemed to dominate as the manager type in the 1960s. However, by the end of the 1970s new corporate executives combined many gamesman traits with characteristics of the company man (Maccoby 1977).

Some decades later, Maccoby (2000) developed four types of leaders based on Freud's distinctions between erotic, obsessive, and narcissistic personalities. These are:

- The authoritarian type, who excels in traits of character such as tidiness, thriftiness, stubbornness, but also in the ability to switch between being active and passive, as well as in giving orders or disobeying.
- The narcissistic type, who excels in a high degree of self-satisfaction with respect to pride, is focused solely on self-preservation, but at the same time is highly aggressive, wants to impress others, and is therefore suitable as leader.
- The narcissistic-coercive type, who combines thoroughness with narcissistic self-confidence.
- The erotic-narcissistic type, who seeks love and affection.

According to Maccoby, the narcissistic type and the narcissistic-coercive type are most likely to correspond with the general understanding of a great leader. This opinion is supported by an earlier notion of Kets de Vries (1989), who sees espe-cially the narcissistic personality as preferable leader personality. Leaders with such a personality develop clear visions, want to change the existing rules, and are able to attract followers. According to Kets de Vries (2004, p. 188), "a solid dose of narcissism is a prerequisite for anyone who hopes to rise to the top of an organiza-tion." Cluley's (2008) thoughts on the relation between groups and leadership, drawing back to Freud's ideas of identification and idealization, might provide an explanation for that. Narcissistic leaders, with, for example, their sense of self-importance and preoccupation with fantasies of unlimited success

(Sankowsky 1995), appear to followers as being completely free from social influences. In this sense, they are perceived as standing above the group, i.e., outside the frame of the social entity. They seem not to be influenced by any social context but act as an independent individual that embodies the ideal of followers.

Selected Pros and Cons

The main advantages of the psychodynamic leadership approach are the focus on relationships and its universal application (Stech 2004). Additionally, providing basic psychological explanations for the emergence of leaders could be regarded as another positive aspect in this concept.

The analysis of leadership reality takes into account the complexity of leadership relations, or in other words "the intricate playing field between leader and followers" (Kets de Vries 2004, p. 185). Needs and emotions of leaders as well as of followers are considered which positively distinguish this approach from general leadership research where emotions are often neglected (Gibb 1958). The relationship between leader and followers results from a mixture of conscious as well as unconscious needs and emotions.

Applying this theoretical leadership approach allows analyzing most versatile leadership relations in many different forms of organizations. As this theory is based on the universal concepts of depth psychology its explanatory capability is not limited to corporations.

As a final advantage, the psychodynamic leadership approach offers explanations of the basic process of leader emergence. Drawing on experiences made in early childhood and adolescence but also using the model of projective identification this approach provides a fundamental outline for the emergence and existence of leaders. This idea has been later adopted by some scholars of the charismatic leadership approach in order to explicate the emergence of charismatic leaders.

A disadvantage of this approach is the neglect of situational aspects to a large extent. In whatever specific organizational contexts, leadership always emerges based on early experiences made in childhood and adolescence. Moreover, leaders and followers behave according to these experiences and the resulting internalized patterns of leadership behavior. Therefore, the psychodynamic leadership approach has some parallels with the classical trait approach, explaining behavior exclusively by considering the personality structure of the participants but, however, not recognizing situational differences.

In addition to that, the transfer of results of clinical psychology, which are often strongly influenced by the bias of the researcher and psychodynamic assumptions, to "normal" behavior of executives and staff seems to be problematic (Stech 2004). The terms, hypotheses, and models which are used in this regard are in most cases applied independently from their theoretical preconditions and, hence, even intensify the difficulty of transference.

Chapter 5
Neocharismatic Leadership

Introduction and Background

The neocharismatic leadership approach basically deals with the process of change and consequently the transformation of followers. This process contains charismatic and visionary aspects which are especially understood as located in the characteristics and subsequent patterns of behavior of the leading person. "(Leadership) must be visionary; it must transform those who see the vision, and give them a new and stronger sense of purpose and meaning" (Van Seters and Field 1990, p. 38). Resulting from that idea the main research focus of scholars adopting the perspective of this theoretical approach is on how to distinguish charismatic from "ordinary" leaders and on how charismatic or transformational leaders affect followers.

The neocharismatic leadership research can be divided into several approaches (e.g., House et al. 1998; Bryman 1992; Yukl 2006). The syllable "neo" in the title of this theoretical approach means, firstly, that this research is advancing explicitly or implicitly the early charisma concept of Max Weber and, secondly, that the concept of charisma is now applied to private organizations in addition to its early application to religious or political movements.

Bryman (1992) introduced a popular distinction of the approach. He classified the neocharismatic leadership approach into charismatic leadership (e.g., House 1977; Conger and Kanungo 1987; Shamir et al. 1993; House et al. 1998, 1999; Howell and Shamir 2005), transformational leadership (e.g., Bass 1995; Avolio and Bass 1987), and visionary leadership (e.g., Bennis and Nanus 1985). The following description only partly follows the distinction introduced. Instead, the chapter will particularly focus on the approaches initiated by House and Bass, that is, charismatic leadership and transformational leadership. The perspective of visionary leadership is disregarded because this approach is later on absorbed by the other approaches. At first, however, I will outline the basic concept of charisma developed by Max Weber (1968).

I. Winkler, *Contemporary Leadership Theories*, Contributions to Management Science,
DOI 10.1007/978-3-7908-2158-1_5, © Springer-Verlag Berlin Heidelberg 2010

Max Weber: Charisma and Legitimated Authority

Max Weber – probably one of the most famous German Sociologists – in one of his main works dealt with the issues of power, domination, legitimated action, and authority. He highlighted three basic types of legitimate authority within a society: traditional authority, legal or traditional authority, and charismatic authority (Weber 1968, for an overview see also Ritzer 2007).

Traditional authority means that traditional rights of a powerful and dominant individual or group are accepted by subordinates. Traditional authority is based on the belief that traditional rules and powers are true and effective. The dominant individual could be a priest, clan leader, head of the family, or some other patriarch. Rational or legal authority rests on a belief in the legality of enacted rules and the right of those elevated to authority under such rules to issue commands (Gingrich 1999). In modern societies, authority is in large part exercised on the basis of bureaucracy. According to Weber, the dominant tendency for organizations was to become more routinized, rational, and bureaucratic. As a consequence, rational and legal types of authority became more dominant. Charismatic authority – the type of authority most important for this chapter – rests on "devotion to the exceptional sanctity, heroism, or exemplary character of an individual and of the normative patterns or order revealed or ordained by him" (Weber 1968, p. 215). Charisma is defined as the quality of an individual's personality that is considered extraordinary, and followers may consider this quality to be endowed with supernatural, superhuman, or exceptional powers or qualities (Gingrich 1999). Weber (1968) also points to the fact that charisma is an ascribed feature. If followers define a leader as charismatic, then he or she is likely to be a charismatic leader irrespective of whether he or she actually possesses any outstanding traits.

Charismatic Leadership

Charismatic leadership as theoretical leadership approach today could be considered as the most influential approach on leadership research. In the following sections relevant developmental steps of the theory are presented.

The Early Concept

In his early contribution – which could be considered as the basic work of the charismatic leadership approach – House (1977) revised charismatic leadership in the literature of sociological and political sciences and reflected on Weber's conception of charisma. From that, he developed a first theoretical framework including the characteristics of charismatic leaders, the behavior of charismatic leaders, the effects of charismatic leadership, and the social determinants of charismatic leadership.

On the one hand, House (1977) explains the specific effects charismatic leadership has on followers with particular individual characteristics a leader has, such as, dominance, self-security, a need to influence others, and a strong conviction in the moral integrity of his/her belief. On the other hand, charismatic leaders show specific patterns of behavior. They act, for example, as a strong role model, they articulate ideological goals that have strong moral overtones, or they encourage task-oriented motives of followers with the help of power or appreciation.

As a third feature of charismatic leadership, House (1977) highlights two conditions which favor the development of charismatic leadership. Firstly, the existence of a crisis situation is considered important for the emergence of a charismatic leader. If in such a situation a person with the above-mentioned characteristics and patterns of behavior appears, there is a high probability that this person is acknowledged as a charismatic leader. Secondly, the opportunity to articulate an ideological goal for a person to have charismatic effects is assumed to be a situational requirement. This need of an opportunity for a person to articulate a vision has been neglected in later writings on this theory.

Regarding the effects of charismatic leadership House (1977) emphasizes that charismatic leaders increase follower commitment, follower motivation, and follower performance by, for example, developing followers' trust in the correctness of the leader's beliefs, creating emotional involvement for the followers in the mission, or arousing a feeling on the part of the followers that they will be able to contribute to the mission.

Charisma as Attribution

Conger and Kanungo (1987) advanced the early concept of House on the basis of their own empirical investigations. They focused on the aspect of attribution which has been neglected in the early works of House. Conger and Kanungo demonstrate that charisma is not a mystic quality of a person but is ascribed to the individual as a result of his/her behavior or mere physical presence. Hence, charismatic leadership or a charismatic leader emerges when people are ascribing a person certain charismatic qualities based on his/her behavior during a crisis (Boal and Bryson 1987). House also points out in later works that charisma cannot be found exclusively in the characteristics of the leader but is also sought in the relationship between leader and follower. Therefore, the follower has an important role in regard to the development of a charismatic leadership relation (e.g., Klein and House 1995).

According to Conger and Kanungo (1987, 1988) and Conger (1989), the attribution of charisma to leaders depends on four variables:

1. The degree of discrepancy between the status quo and the future goal or vision advocated by the leader.
2. The use of innovative and unconventional means for achieving the desired change.

3. A realistic assessment of environmental resources and constraints for bringing about such change.
4. The nature of articulation and impression management employed to inspire subordinations in the pursuit of the vision.

The development and the articulation of a vision are considered to be the main issues for the attribution of charisma in this concept. "The more idealized the future goals advocated by the leader, the more discrepant they become in relation to the status quo, and the greater the discrepancy of the goal from the status quo, the more likely is the attribution that the leader has extraordinary vision, not just ordinary goals" (Conger and Kanungo 1988, p. 157). Following the idea of charisma as an attribution Steyrer (1998) developed a charisma model based on social-cognitive information processing. In his model, Steyrer followed the idea of leadership archetypes and developed four different phenotypes, which are the hero (heroic charisma), the father (paternalistic charisma), the savior (missionary charisma), and the king (majestic charisma). Depending on the prototypicality of leader behavior in followers' perception, different kinds of charisma are attributed.

Self-Concept-Based Theory of Charisma

The next important stage of the approach has been the development of the self-concept-based theory of charismatic leadership. Shamir et al. (1993) raised the problem that previous work on charismatic leadership does not provide an explanation of the process by which charismatic leadership has its profound effects. So far only types of change have been emphasized, e.g., charismatic leaders raise followers to higher levels of morality. However, no motivational explanations are provided, to explain how charismatic leaders bring about changes in followers' values, goals, needs, and aspirations. The authors conclude that influences on followers' self-concept are key here. By effectively linking followers' self-concept to the mission, charismatic leaders are able to increase the intrinsic value of followers' efforts and goals. The behavioral patterns of charismatic leaders in order to effect these efforts and goals are, first, behavior that emphasizes collective values and ideologies, and that links the mission, goals, and expected behavior to follower's values and ideologies; second, behavior that emphasizes the collective identity of the organization and that links the mission, goals, and expected behaviors to this identity; and, third, leader behavior displaying personal commitment to the values, identities, and goals which he or she stands for and promotes.

Charisma as Fire

Klein and House (1995) summarized the then current stand of development of the theory by employing a fire metaphor (see Fig. 1).

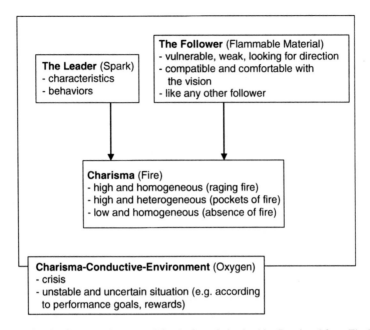

Fig. 1 Applying the fire-metaphor to explain charismatic leadership (Reprinted from The Leadership Quarterly, 6/2, Klein, K.J. & House, R.J., On fire: Charismatic leadership and levels of analysis, p. 186, Copyright (1995), with permission from Elsevier)

The charisma-conductive environment serves as oxygen. Such environment could be found in times of crises or any other unstable and uncertain situation. In such contexts, leaders with specific charismatic characteristics and behaviors serve as the spark. Followers though are seen as flammable material. Here different authors develop different perspectives on the nature of this flammable material. Some see followers as vulnerable, weak, and searching for direction in times of a crisis. Others highlight the fact that followers have to perceive the proposed vision of the leader as compatible to their own goals and, hence, feel comfortable with it. Yet, another group of scholars thinks that any kind of follower is susceptible for charismatic leadership. If the spark comes into contact with the flammable material, then this material is set on fire, meaning charisma or, in other words, charismatic leadership emerges. Here, Klein and House suggest different kinds of fire. If there is a strong attribution of charismatic qualities to a leader by all members of a group, then the authors speak of raging fire. If there is a strong attribution but only by some followers, then the result is so-called pockets of fire, i.e., some members of the group or some groups within an organization perceive and accept the leader as a charismatic one. If, however, there is only low attribution of charisma to the leader but by all members of a group, then no fire gets sparked.

Value-Based Leadership

Later on, House and colleagues distanced themselves from the term "charismatic" and called their approach "value-based leadership" (House et al. 1998). "Value-based leadership is defined as a relationship between an individual (leader) and one or more followers based on shared strongly internalized ideological values espoused by the leader and strong follower identification with these values" (House et al. 1998, p. 2). The authors pointed to the problematic impression with the attribute "charismatic" as a person who is charming, attractive, and sometimes macho, and sexually appealing. They demonstrate, however, that charismatic leadership is enacted (a) by leaders with a more emotionally expressive behavior (e.g., John F. Kennedy) and/or (b) with a nonemotionally expressive behavior (e.g., Nelson Mandela). It is assumed that ideological values, which are values concerning what is morally right and wrong (e.g., in terms of personal moral responsibility, concern for honesty, fairness, and meeting obligations to others such as followers), resonate with the deeply held values and emotions of followers. According to the authors, value-based leaders infuse collectives, organizations, and work with ideological values by articulating an ideological vision, a vision of a better future on which followers claim to have a moral right. In other words: ". . . the leader empowers followers and guides them towards a moral ideal" (Jordan 1998, p. 2). Examples of ideological values in visions are a challenging or rewarding work environment, freedom from highly controlling rules, fairness, or high quality of services and products (House et al. 1998). It is up to the leader to articulate a vision that is consistent with the collective identity of the followers and that creates emotional and motivational commitment. The expected results of value-based leadership on the side of the followers are, however, quite similar to earlier expressions of effects of charismatic leadership. So, expected results comprise, firstly, the exceptionally strong identification of followers with the leader, the collective vision formulated by the leader, and the collective. Secondly, an internalized commitment to the vision of the leader and to the collective is assumed. Thirdly, followers' motives should be awakened that are relevant to the accomplishment of the collective vision. Fourthly, the development of follower willingness is expected to extend effort above and beyond the call of duty.

Back to the Followers

Recently, Howell and Shamir (2005) pointed to the fact that charismatic leadership theories basically focus on leader qualities and behaviors. Followers are often understood as being in a rather passive role waiting to be inspired and motivated by the charismatic leader. Thus, they suggest to refocus on the role of followers and to understand charisma as a relationship that is jointly produced by leaders and followers (see also Campbell et al. 2008). Their basic assumption is that depending on their self-concept followers are developing two different types of charismatic leadership with the leader, i.e., personalized and socialized. Howell and Shamir propose that two characteristics of followers' self-concepts determine the nature of the charismatic relationship with the leader, the so-called self-concept clarity, defined as the extent to which the contents of the individuals' self-concept are clearly and confidentially defined, and the core level of self-identity, which could be individualistic, relational or collective.

If followers have a low self-concept clarity and, thus, no clear and consistent self-concept guiding their behavior, then they are open to offers from attractive and powerful others providing direction. Such followers look for charismatic leaders and identify strongly with such a leader, which results in a personalized charismatic relationship. Followers having a high self-concept clarity and, thus, a high motivation for self-expression as well as a high motivation to protect and enhance their high self-esteem are more open to leaders who link goals and required behavior to valued components of the followers' self-concept. The resulting leader–follower relation – termed socialized charismatic relationship – is based on the ability of the leader to show how his/her mission reflects the identities and values of the follower.

Regarding the core level of self-identity, individualistic people focus on personal interest and are less likely to form a charismatic relationship (Howell and Shamir 2005). Individuals with a relational self-concept orientation define themselves in terms of their relationships with significant others. They seek direction, self-validation, and satisfaction from personal relationships and therefore are likely to form charismatic relationships with attractive or powerful individuals based on personal identification with the leader. Individuals with a collective self-concept orientation define themselves in terms of group achievements and comparisons with other groups. Subsequently, they are likely to form charismatic relationships with a leader who represents and supports the identity and values of the group based on social identification with the group.

The GLOBE Research Program

House further develops the approach of charismatic, and particularly value-based, leadership as well as empirically confirms the relevance of the concept in his Global Leadership and Organizational Behavior Effectiveness (GLOBE) – Research Program (e.g., House et al. 1999; Den Hartog et al., 1999; House et al. 2004). This long-term research program started in 1994 and consists of a network of 170 social scientists and management scholars from over 62 countries. The basic aim is to develop an empirically based theory to describe, understand, and predict the impact of cultural variables on leadership and organizational processes as well as the effectiveness of these processes. The project can be divided into three phases (House and Hanges 2004). In the first phase, a set of scales was developed and validated that were required for testing the constructs in the conceptual model of the project. In the second phase, some of the propositions specified in the conceptual

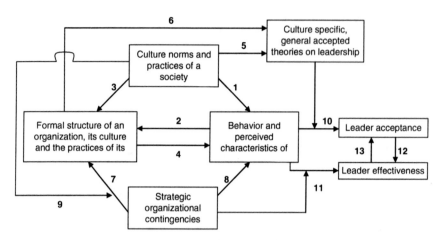

Fig. 2 Theoretical model of GLOBE (Reprinted from House, R.J., Hanges, P.J., Ruiz-Quintanilla, S.A., Dorfman, P.W., Javidan, M., Dickson, M.W., Gupta, V., GLOBE (1999). Cultural influences on leadership and organizations: Project GLOBE. In W.H. Mobley, M.J. Gessner, V. Arnold (Eds.), Advances in global leadership. Stamford, CN: JAI-Press, with permission from Elsevier)

model were empirically tested. The current, third phase empirically tests the parts of the conceptual model concerned with the relations of observed CEO leadership behavior, culturally endorsed implicit leadership theories, leadership acceptance, as well as leadership and organizational effectiveness. As the book at hand is concerned with leadership theories, the subsequent presentation will concentrate on the theoretical assumptions as well as the theoretical model of the GLOBE research program.

The theoretical model is based on previous ideas of the charismatic leadership approach; however, it also extends this theoretical concept. The central theoretical proposition argues that attributes of a culture are predictive of the practices of organizations and leader attributes and behaviors that are most frequently enacted, acceptable, and effective in that culture (House et al. 1999). Societal culture and organizational form, culture, and practices influence the process by which people come to share implicit theories of leadership. Consequently, such implicit leadership theories are understood as culturally endorsed implicit leadership theories (CLT) that differ between cultures. Figure 2 represents the theoretical model of this analysis.

The central assumption of the concept is that the specific features in which cultures differ from each other influence organizational methods and the understanding of relevant leadership characteristics. Furthermore, a culture also determines the displayed, accepted, and effective patterns of behavior of members in organizations. Subsequently, the following assumptions can be made corresponding to the arrows in Fig. 2 (House et al. 1999; House and Javidan 2004):

1. The cultural values of a society and the shared practices of behavior influence the behavior of leaders.

2. Leadership has an influence on formal structures in organizations as well as on their culture and the practices of organizational members. Here, the emphasis is particularly on the influence of the founder.
3. The cultural values of a society and the shared practices of behavior influence the formal structures in organizations, their culture as well as the enacted practices of organizational members. Since organizations are embedded in a particular society they will be influenced by values, norms, and assumptions of this society.
4. The formal structures of an organization, its culture, and the practices of organizational members influence the behavior of leaders. They are committed to a particular behavior (e.g., a particular style of leadership) because of these elements.
5. The culture of a society has an impact on the emergence of CLTs.
6. The formal structures of an organization, its culture, and the practices of its members also influence the development of shared implicit theories of leadership. Consequently, culture-specific, generally accepted implicit theories of leadership develop in the course of time due to the influence of organizational and societal cultures.
7. Strategic organizational contingencies influence the formal structures of an organization as well as its culture and the methods of its members. The size of the company, the applied technology and the entrepreneurial environment are understood as conditions the organization has to adapt to in order to be effective and capable of surviving.
8. Strategic organizational contingencies influence the ideas about relevant leadership characteristics as well as leadership behavior. Leaders are, for example, chosen according to specific criteria which can vary depending on the size of the company or the applied technology.
9. The relationship between strategic organizational contingencies and the structure and culture of an organization as well as the enacted practices of its members is influenced by societal culture. For example, a high degree of insecurity avoidance in a society might be reflected in a high degree of formalization.
10. The acceptance as a leader results from the interaction between culturally accepted implicit theories of leadership and observed leadership characteristics or patterns of behavior. If these characteristics or behavior patterns fit in existing CLTs, the acceptance of a person as a leader increases.
11. The effectiveness of leadership results from the interaction between observed leadership characteristics and patterns of behavior and organizational contingencies. The more leadership behavior orientates itself on the conditions of an organization, the more effective it is.
12. Leader acceptance has an impact on leadership effectiveness. Accepted leaders are able to influence their followers to a higher degree and for a longer period of time.
13. Leadership effectiveness influences leader acceptance. Effective leaders are accepted by all or most followers in the long term, because those followers who do not accept the leader will by and by leave the group or organization.

According to the results of the GLOBE project, charismatic behavior, conceived as visionary, inspirational, self-sacrificing, integrating, determined, and performance-oriented (House et al. 1999), is an element of implicit leadership theories across cultures. Hence, House and colleagues assume a situational independence of charisma as an important element in leadership emergence. Individuals showing accordant charismatic behavior or possessing charismatic characteristics are perceived as leaders in different national cultures.

Transformational Leadership

In 1985, Bass published the basic ideas of the concept of transformational leadership. According to him, leadership research hitherto had only been focusing on exchange relations. With his theoretical approach, Bass aimed at advancing existing research by focusing on the crucial aspect of the transformation of followers because "the real movers and shakers of the world are transformational leaders" (Bass 1982, p. 147). Bass particularly refers to Burns (1978) and his work about political leaders as well as the interaction between leader and follower roles.

Burns (1978) in his work on political leaders introduced the distinction between transactional and transformational leaders as subtypes of the moral leader. Up to now, this distinction is part of the concept of transformational leadership. Transactional leadership refers to exchange theories which deal with any exchange between leader and followers, for example, managers who express monetary rewards for employees' extra performance (Burns 1978; Bass 1985; Northouse 2007). Transactional leaders establish a relation with followers in which exchanging one thing for another is the basic mode of interaction. In contrast, transformational leadership refers to an interaction between leader and followers which considers the needs of the followers (Kezar et al. 2006). Motivation of both leaders and followers is increased, the more developed the relationship becomes. In contrast to the transactional leader, the transformational leader also arouses or changes needs that may have been latent (Bass 1985). With transformational leadership, transactional exchanges take place as well, but higher needs are considered which are necessary for the development of the follower's personality. Transformational leadership is the kind of leadership "where the leader raises the subordinate's level of need (on Maslow's scale) and energizes the subordinate into accomplishments beyond the subordinate's original expectations that may transcend the subordinate's self-interests" (Bass 1982, p. 142, emphasis as original). Within this process, leaders as well as subordinates can experience higher moral values.

The theoretical approach of transformational leadership builds on, but also advances, both Burns' early writings on transactional and transformational leadership and House's concept of charismatic leadership. In contrast to Burns, Bass focused more on followers and highlighted that a leader can be both transactional and transformational (Bryman 1992). Bass also argued that transformational

Transformational Leadership	Transactional Leadership	Non-Leadership
Factor 1: Idealized Influence, Charisma	Factor 5: Contingent Reward	Factor 7: Laissez-faire (non-transactional)
Factor 2: Inspirational Motivation	Factor 6: Management by Exception	
Factor 3: Intellectual Stimulation		
Factor 4: Individualized Consideration		

Fig. 3 Model of the transformational leadership approach (Northouse, P.G. (2004). Leadership. Theory and practice. Thousand Oaks: Sage, p. 175. Copyright 2003 by Sage Publications Inc Books. Reproduced with permission of Sage Publications Inc.)

leadership emerges especially in instable contexts and situations that are perceived as being uncertain and ambiguous. In contrast to the charismatic theory of leadership developed by House (1977), the concept of Bass also addressed emotional elements and regarded charisma as just one particular element of transformational leadership (Avolio and Bass 1987; Bass 1995; Northouse 2004).

The central model of this approach illustrates the differences of transformational and nontransformational leadership behavior (see Fig. 3).

Factors of Transformational Leadership

Factor 1: Charisma and Idealized Influence

This factor describes charismatic leaders who represent a strong role model for subordinates. Followers identify themselves with the high moral and ethical demands of the leader whom they respect and trust. Leaders with charisma are, therefore, regarded as something special. They become a source of inspiration and charismatic identification through their enthusiasm and past accomplishments (Bass 1985). Charismatic leaders have also a sense of vision which should effectively be articulated so that followers can use it as orientation for their behavior (Awamleh and Gardner 1999). According to Avolio and Gardner (2005), the vision should originate from the leader's authenticity in order to "provide the impetus for followers to be more engaged, aware and intelligent about the direction being set so that they can contribute their best views and questions about the desired future state" (Avolio and Gardner 2005, p. 328). If the leader is inauthentic, then at some point the vision might be unmasked as a source of manipulation in order to gain personal objectives, which in turn results in lowered follower commitment and performance (Avolio and Gardner 2005).

Factor 2: Individualized Consideration

Considering individual needs of followers and creating a supportive atmosphere are the basic behavioral patterns of leaders who can be assigned to this factor. Leaders are coaches and advisors and help followers to advance by means of a more participative style of leadership. The individual characteristics of the followers are considered and the leader treats each follower with respect (Avolio and Bass 1987). The leader develops a particular kind of relationship with the followers in which their concerns and needs are understood and shared (Bass and Avolio 1990).

Factor 3: Intellectual Stimulation

Leaders who are ranked among this group encourage their subordinates to be creative and innovative in order to advance their own but also the leader's beliefs and values. Followers are supposed to test new approaches as well as develop new ways of dealing with their working environment. They are supported in questioning their beliefs, assumptions, and values (Bass and Avolio 1990). This factor of transformational leadership encourages followers to participate actively in problem solving.

Factor 4: Inspirational Motivation

This factor addresses leaders who can motivate followers to share their vision and to get involved with this vision. "Team spirit is aroused. Enthusiasm and optimism are displayed" (Bass and Avolio 1994, p. 3). Leaders use symbols and emotional appeals in order to create team spirit and to get their subordinates to reach higher aims, which followers would not be willing to do by virtue of their self-interest. Inspirational leaders communicate high expectations, use symbols to focus followers' efforts, and express important values in simple ways (Bass 1990b).

Factors of Transactional Leadership

Transactional leadership neither focuses on individual characteristics of followers nor supports their individual development. It is rather concerned with the exchange relationship between leader and follower in which both search for their individual benefits. Subordinates follow leaders only because they expect benefits and try to avoid punishment. Two factors are to be considered as being at "the heart of what is called transactional leadership" (Podsakoff et al. 2006, p. 114): compensation for followers' performance, labeled contingent reward, and methods of active and passive corrective transactions, labeled management-by-exception.

Factor 5: Contingent Reward

Leaders reward followers' good performance. This factor of transactional leadership addresses means of positive reinforcement used by the leader to ensure a certain level of performance of the followers. The leader monitors followers' behavior and offers financial as well as nonfinancial rewards (Kirkbride 2006). The followers show good performance because they usually expect a material (financial) reward.

Factor 6: Management-by-Exception

This factor of transactional leadership focuses on negative reinforcement. Active management-by-exception means that the leader closely monitors followers' behavior and immediately and directly intervenes in case of mistakes or poor performance. In the case of passive management-by exception, the leader only interferes with passive corrective actions if behavior or performance standards are not met by the followers. In both cases, the leader uses corrective criticism, gives negative feedback, or applies other kinds of negative reinforcement (Northouse 2007).

Non-leadership

Factor 7: Laissez-faire

This factor addresses the absence of leadership. As the French phrase "laissez-faire" already indicates, the leader abstains from doing anything. The leader takes no responsibility, makes no decisions, and gives no feedback or support to followers. In short, the leader is letting things slide without intervening.

Effects of Transformational Leadership

Besides describing the difference between transactional and transformational leadership, research also concentrates on the effects of transformational leadership. According to Bass (1985), Bass and Avolio (1990), Bass and Avolio (1994), and many other authors working in this field, transformational leadership results in performance beyond expectations (see Fig. 4).

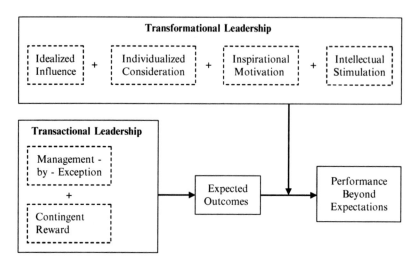

Fig. 4 The effect of transformational leadership (adapted from Bass, B.M., & Avolio, B.J. (1990). The implications of transactional and transformational leadership for individual, team, and organizational development. In W.A. Pasmore, & R.W. Woodman (Eds.), Research in Organizational Change and Development. Greenwich, CT: JAI Press, p. 237)

Transactional leaders produce sufficient confidence in followers and support them in completing their tasks. They recognize followers' needs and desires but also clarify how those needs will be fulfilled if followers show the expected performance. However, transactional leadership can be satisfying and effective only in a limited way. Instead, transformational leadership adds substantially to the impact of transactional leadership (Bass 1998). Because of the ineffectiveness of contingent negative reinforcement and several other reasons, transactional leadership is regarded as resulting in expected performance with little possibility to reach significant improvements in effort and outcome (Bass and Avolio 1990). Transformational leadership, in contrast, results in more extensive changes according to effort, performance, and development. "Transformational leaders establish goals and objectives for performance while also emphasizing that followers should take more responsibility as appropriate, systematically assuming greater leadership responsibilities" (Bass and Avolio 1990, p. 241). Consequently, transformational leadership goes beyond the understanding of the leader's function to simply getting the job done by guiding the followers (Bass and Avolio 1994). Outcomes due to transformational leadership exceed expectations as followers show extraordinary performance. After reviewing numerous studies in the field of transformational leadership, Bass (1999) stated empirical evidence for the proposed differences in effectiveness. He put it as follows: "The transformational factors are usually found more highly correlated with outcomes in effectiveness and satisfaction of colleagues than is contingent reward. Contingent reward is ordinarily more highly correlated with outcomes than is managing-by-exception, particularly passive managing by-exception. Finally, laissez-faire leadership is almost uniformly negatively correlated with outcomes" (Bass 1999, p. 22).

Similarities in the Approaches

Recapitulating the description of the two main theoretical streams of neo-charismatic leadership, two similarities could be highlighted. Accordingly, Bass stated that "there is some overlap between the transformational and the charismatic leader" (Bass 1982, p. 150). In particular, both approaches are similar in their reference to the concept of charisma, which makes a sharp distinction difficult (Bryman 1992), especially regarding the more recent developments of the approaches. Even if Bass and Avolio (1993) stated that charisma and transformational leadership cannot be used synonymously, they admit that in their empirical results "charisma accounted for the largest amount of variance in ratings associated with transformational leadership" (Bass and Avolio 1993, p. 62). Furthermore, they found out that the three, other factors of transformational leadership tend to highly correlate with charisma. Additionally, both concepts suggest that charismatic or transformational leaders are more likely to emerge in times of crisis and change.

A basic, probably fundamental difference between the approaches is highlighted by Hughes et al. (1996). They point out that considering the needs of the followers is understood as an important difference between the transformational and the charismatic leadership approach. The former is based on values of the followers whereas the latter is based on values of the charismatic leader.

Selected Pros and Cons

On the positive side, neo-charismatic leadership theory explains why charismatic/transformational leaders are apparently more successful, in terms of followers' performance and satisfaction. This aspect has been proven in several empirical studies which show a significant link between the factor "charisma," on the one hand, and employees' perceived efficiency and satisfaction, on the other hand (e.g., Howell and Avolio 1993; Barling et al. 1996; Kirkpatrick and Locke 1996; Sosik et al. 1997). Furthermore, the approach demonstrates that employees in times of crises or transformation are more likely to attribute leadership to individuals perceived as charismatic.

A first problem regarding this theory concerns the qualities of the leader as "great man," "social architect," or "elitist player" which are generally overemphasized (Shamir 1999). Hence, it appears that the classical trait approach is revived, especially in early works. In these studies, "charisma would seem to be something that you either have or do not have, like brown hair, or an introverted personality, or an IQ of 142" (Bryman 1992, p. 43). It is partly neglected that leadership is attributed to a person due to characteristics and behavior perceived as charismatic. Related to that, leaders are often understood as heroes, whereas effective performance of a group or organization depends on the leadership of one person (Yukl 1999).

Secondly, charismatic characteristics of leaders and the resulting behavior are generally assigned to have the most important influence on leadership success. This assumption results in a suppression of organizational and other contextual factors (Yukl and Howell 1999). Ropo and Hunt (1999) go so far as to state that "new leadership often has been abstracted from its contextual settings and investigated in reductionist terms" (Ropo and Hunt 1999, p. 170). That means, even if the early works of House (1977) as well as Bass (1985) emphasized that charismatic and transformational leadership are more likely to be successful in times of change and discontinuity, these contextual limitations are sometimes neglected nowadays (see Beyer 1999; Yukl 1999 for related comments). In this regard, Barbuto (1997) raises a general doubt that charisma is the source for leadership success in non-transformational situations as well.

Thirdly, it stands out that the scholars of the theory are almost exclusively arguing positively. Possible negative motives of charismatic leaders as well as potential problematic effects of charismatic and transformational leadership are partially neglected (Beyer 1999). That these effects exist is, for example, shown by Yukl's (1994) comments on the dark side of charisma as well as by the study of Dorian et al. (2000) about the negative effects of a charismatic leader of a work group in a psychiatric clinic. To provide an example, the approach to some extent implies a certain dependence of followers on the leader. This dependence often becomes evident when the charismatic leader is leaving the group (Bryman 1992). As this theory is strongly bounded to the person of the leader, it could be expected that problems, like the loss of orientation, will occur among followers if the leader leaves or is exchanged.

Fourthly, a last point of criticism addresses the temporal stability of charismatic leadership and to some extent transformational leadership. Since charismatic characteristics are assigned by the followers, the behavior of the leader has to allow a permanent reproduction of these attributions. Consequently, the charismatic leader must continue to demonstrate his/her effectiveness. Actions attributed to the leader have to continue to benefit the organization and followers, no matter whether their efficiency is real or just apparent (Bass 1985). If the leader "fails to benefit his followers, it is likely that his charismatic authority will disappear" (Weber 1968, p. 242). Research on charismatic and transformational leadership, however, has only to some extent started to address this problem.

Chapter 6
Leader–Member Exchange Theory

Introduction and Background

The Leader–Member Exchange (LMX) theory first emerged in the 1970s. It conceptualizes leadership as a process of interaction between leader and follower and centers on the dyadic exchange relationships between both. The leader–follower relationships within work groups are split up into a set of working relationships between a leader and the various members of the work team (Van Breukelen et al. 2006) since it is assumed that different relationships between the leader and every single follower develop. Hence, the leader may have different types of transactions and different kinds of relations with different followers (Van Seters and Field 1990). "For example, each superior may offer one subordinate a substantial amount of interpersonal support and attention ... while at the same time he or she offers a second subordinate less support" (Dansereau et al. 1982, p. 84). Following Blau's (1964) writings on social and economic exchange, LMX theory assumes that leaders and followers are involved in an exchange relationship. Followers follow because they receive something from the leader. In turn, leaders lead as they get something from followers (Messick 2004). Hence, the quality of the exchange relationship is the basic unit of analysis (Van Breukelen et al. 2006). The theoretical approach basically grounds in the writings of Graen (1976), Dansereau et al. (1975), as well as Graen and Cashman (1975). To date, the theory has undergone several stages of development; a first stage where the idea of vertical dyadic linkages was elaborated, a second stage that concentrated on the effects of linkages regarding different exchange qualities, a third stage that deals with the development of dyadic leader–member exchange relationships (the life cycle of leadership making), and a fourth and so far final stage that expands the ideas of the concept to groups and networks (Graen and Uhl-Bien 1995). This chapter does not follow this four-stage development but offers a simpler division into early studies on LMX theory, reflecting the first and second stages described by Graen and Uhl-Bien, and later publications, demonstrating the normative turn in the theory, and

I. Winkler, *Contemporary Leadership Theories*, Contributions to Management Science, 47
DOI 10.1007/978-3-7908-2158-1_6, © Springer-Verlag Berlin Heidelberg 2010

concentrating on the development of high-quality leader–member exchange relations (see also Northouse 2004).

Qualities and Development of Leader–Member Relations

Early work on LMX theory, at that time also called Vertical Dyad Linkage Theory, focused on the description of the vertical relationships between a superior and his inferiors. Two kinds of relationships between leader and followers have been identified. One is based on formal relationships within the employment contract and the formal role definition (named "low-quality leader–member relations"), and the other is founded on extended and negotiated role responsibilities and includes trust, respect, and mutual influence (named "high-quality leader–member relations"). The superior is having formal relationships with members of the so-called "out-group" and extended relationships with the so-called "in-group" (see Fig. 1).

Members of a group become part of the "in-group" or "out-group" in the leader–follower relationship already at an early stage of group membership. This distinction depends on how the relationship with the superior during the mutual role definition develops and how the participants assess the potential advantages and costs of the relationship. Personality and other personal characteristics play an important role here (Dansereau et al. 1975), as these aspects influence the behavior and attitudes of both the superior and the subordinate. Becoming a member of one or the other group depends on the behavior of the subordinate concerning the extent to which he/she is expanding the responsibility within the leader–follower relationship. The higher the willingness to contribute to the aim of the group beyond the formal role determined by the work contract and the hierarchy, the more a subordinate becomes part of the "in-group." As a consequence, the mutual relationships between leader and follower include more than just formal aspects, but also trust, loyalty, and mutual influence. If a follower is not interested in assuming such enlarged responsibilities, he/she will become a member of the "out-group."

Dienesch and Liden (1986) proposed a process model of the development of a particular relationship quality (see Fig. 2). They included leader and member characteristics as well as ideas from attribution theory. According to Van Breukelen

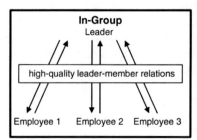 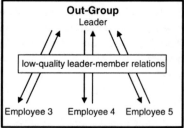

Fig. 1 "In-group" and "out-group" relationships. Adapted from Northouse (2004, p. 150)

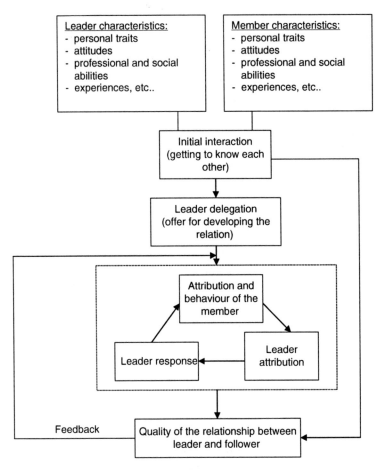

Fig. 2 LMX development process (adapted from Dienesch, R. M., & Liden, R. C. (1986). Leader-Member exchange model of leadership: A critique and further development. Academy of Management Review, 11(3), p. 627. Copyright 1986 by Academy of Management (NY). Reproduced with permission of Academy of Management (NY).)

et al. (2006), there is evidence that a certain quality of the relationships forms rather quickly, i.e., often within a few weeks after the first encounter.

The figure illustrates that both participants of the leader–member dyad posses their own characteristics, attitudes, professional and social abilities, as well as former experiences. These aspects strongly influence the interaction between leader and follower and, therefore, the future quality of the relationship. Particularly for members, Epitropaki and Martin (2005) have shown that the leader's match with members' implicit leadership theories (ILT) has an important influence on LMX quality.

In the Dienesch and Liden model, the initial interactions between both participants are of specific importance. During these early encounters the members of the dyad receive a first impression of each other. According to a recent study by Nahrgang et al. (2009), in the early stages of the interaction, member extraversion (e.g., being participative or enthusiastic) seems to influence the initial quality of the exchange from the leader's perspective. From the member's point of view, it is leader agreeableness (e.g., being trusting or cooperative) that influences the initial LMX quality. The initial impression in the early encounters, however, can also be influenced by stereotypes and rather quick judgments, which may also have a direct effect on the quality of the relationship (see the direct arrow from "initial interaction" to "quality of relationship"). Based on this effect, the attribution process can be entirely "bypassed", meaning the leader makes an immediate judgment about the follower (Dienesch and Liden 1986).

In the course of development of the relationship, the leader offers the follower a collaboration that goes beyond formal role relations or, as Dienesch and Liden (1986, p. 629) name it, "an initial set of duties." This offer can be regarded as a trial offer by the leader in order to test the follower. It results in a particular behavior of the subordinate which is affected by the following considerations:

- How does the follower want to present himself/herself to the leader?
- In which way and how much does the follower benefit from accepting the offer?
- Is it possible to say from the way the offer was made whether the superior wants to exploit the follower or if he/she sees the follower as an equal partner?
- What impression does the follower have from the leader due to past interaction?

Based on the results of these considerations, the follower shows subsequent behavior, which is then perceived and interpreted by the leader. The superior evaluates the reaction of the follower by mentally ascribing particular causes. Dienesch and Liden do not further describe this attribution process but refer directly to the ideas of attribution theory (see also Steiner 1997 for an explanation of this process). The reaction of the leader depends on the possible cause he or she attributes to the follower's behavior. With positive conclusions the follower will be included in further actions to build up a closer relationship. In contrast, due to negative interpretations the prospective collaboration with the follower will be restricted to relations within the formal role definition. In the model proposed by Dienesch and Liden, the result of the circle containing behavior, assessment, and subsequent behavior determines the quality of the relationship between the leader and follower.

The feedback arrow demonstrates that the relationship between the members of the dyad is characterized by constant reciprocal actions and reactions as well as related attributions. Hence, the quality of the relationship is not to be conceived as fixed but as constantly developing.

Regarding the particular quality of the relationship between the leader and a member, different authors propose different features. The following are some examples:

- The degree of trust between leader and follower (Liden and Graen 1980)
- The competence of the inferior (Liden and Graen 1980)
- The degree of loyalty between leader and follower (Dansereau et al. 1975)
- The degree of perceived harmony in the relationship (Hollander 1980)
- The degree of reciprocity (Sparrowe and Liden 1997)

- The degree of reciprocal influence (Yukl 1994)
- The extent of interpersonal attraction (Dansereau et al. 1975).

Dienesch and Liden (1986), however, criticize the different criteria regarding a certain "lack of theory." Referring to social exchange theory, the underlying socio- logical theory of the LMX approach, they suggest the following variables influen- cing the quality of the leader–member relation: (a) perceived contribution to the exchange, defined as the perceived amount, direction, and quality each member contributes to mutual objectives; (b) loyalty, defined as the perceived expression of support for the goals and the personal character of the other member of the dyad; and (c) affect, defined as the perceived interpersonal attraction of the members of the dyad. Applying these variables it is argued that it is possible to cover the mutuality of the exchange relationship between the members of a dyad as the most central theoretical focus. Dienesch and Liden (1986, p. 624) claim that "mutuality implies that an exchange must develop along dimensions to which both parties can contrib- ute and that are valued by both parties." Liden and Maslyn (1998) provided empiri- cal support for these variables and developed a fourth one, labeled professional respect. Professional respect includes the perception of the degrees by which each member of the dyad has built a reputation within and/or outside the organization.

Recently, Schyns et al. (2008) proposed that the perceived LMX quality is not only related to the current quality of the relationship. Furthermore, followers' expectancies and preferences play an important role in evaluating the quality of the relation with the leader. Additionally, leaders and members might differ in their cognitive representation of the exchange experiences, which results in different aspects employed when they evaluate LMX quality (Huang et al. 2008).

Effects and Development of High-quality Leader–Member Relationships

Later publications on LMX theory focus less on the description and explanation of the dyadic relation and more on the organizational effectiveness of leader– follower relationships. The extent to which the quality of LMX relationships influences the results for leaders, followers, groups, and organizations as a whole has been analyzed (Graen and Uhl-Bien 1995). Four outcomes which have been analyzed intensively by leadership researchers working in the field of LMX are:

- Satisfaction with the leader as well as general satisfaction (e.g., Liden and Graen 1980; Duchon et al. 1986; Liden and Maslyn 1998; Schyns and Croon 2006)
- Turnover (e.g., Dansereau et al. 1975; Sparrowe 1994; Liden and Maslyn 1998)
- Performance (e.g., Liden and Graen 1980; Duarte et al. 1994; Settoon et al. 1996; Henderson et al. 2008)
- Commitment (e.g., Duchon et al. 1986; Green et al. 1996; Henderson et al. 2008).

The results generally demonstrate that high-quality relationships lead to an increased job satisfaction, a decrease in employee turnover, a more positive assessment of performance, a higher organizational commitment, a better attitude toward work, and a higher proportion of participation (Liden et al. 1993; Graen and Uhl-Bien 1995; Gerstner and Day 1997; Van Breukelen et al. 2006).

As a consequence, it is proposed that leaders should establish positive work relationships ("in-group" relationships) in order to gain advantages for the organization and its members. According to Bauer and Green (1996), the delegation of responsibility rather early in the leader–member relationship as well as allowing employees behavioral freedom is the best way to develop high-quality relationships. Graen and Uhl-Bien (1991) developed a three-stage process of development from formal ("low-quality") to partner ("high-quality") relationships (see Fig. 3).

Within the *first* stage ("stranger phase") the leader–follower relationship is principally restricted to relationships based on the work contract and the formal organizational role. Leaders and followers do not go beyond their organizational roles and have typical "out-group" relations in which the followers just pursue their self-interest. The *second* stage ("acquaintance phase") starts with an offer made by the leader or the follower to expand their relationship beyond the formal contract. Within this stage the follower takes more responsibility, has access to more information, and is developing a stronger personal relationship with his/her superior, whereas the leader opens up further opportunities for the follower's self-development. This stage could be considered as a test of the follower undertaken by the leader in

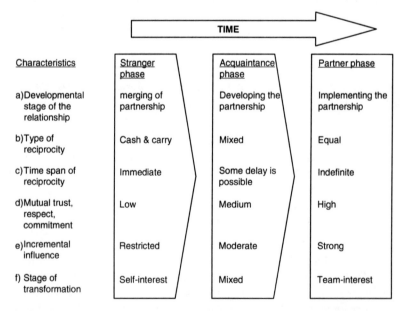

Fig. 3 Life circle of leadership making (Reprinted from The Leadership Quarterly, 6/2, Graen, G. B. & Uhl-Bien, M., Relationship-based approach to leadership: Development of leader-member exchange (LMX) theory of leadership over 25 years: Applying a multi-level multi-domain perspective, p. 231, Copyright (1995), with permission from Elsevier)

order to find out whether this new relationship is wanted. The third stage ("partner phase") is characterized by a high-quality relationship between leader and follower, with the follower being a member of the "in-group." The relationship is based on mutual trust and acknowledgment and rather serves the welfare of the group than the fulfillment of self-interest.

Overall, it becomes obvious that LMX theory has developed from a descriptive to a prescriptive approach (Northouse 1997). Based on the results of empirical research it is assumed that "in-group" relationships are more effective for superiors, inferiors, work groups, and the whole organization.

Selected Pros and Cons

The first positive aspect that has to be mentioned is the extensive descriptive content of the approach regarding leadership processes. Especially the distinction that leaders are having a closer relationship with some of their followers ("in-group") and a more formal one with others ("out-group") is linked to experiences made with leadership reality. LMX theory also provides clear reasons for this distinction. A second positive feature is the focus of analyzing the interaction relationships and, hence, highlighting the important role of communication in leadership (Northouse 1997). Here, communication is defined in a broad sense and includes behavior. The third positive factor is that the results of LMX theory (at least regarding the public sector) are well supported by empirical evidence (see, for example, the overviews by Dienesch and Liden 1986; Liden et al. 1993; Graen and Uhl-Bien 1995).

There are also some negative aspects to mention. For example, there has been criticism about the rather vague division into high-quality and low-quality relationships (e.g., Dienesch and Liden 1986; Sparrowe and Liden 1997) and even more about the not yet fully elaborated prescriptive aspects of the theory. Generally speaking, the argumentations of this approach are a bit shallow. Firstly, possible undesired or unintended effects separating employees into "in-group" and "out-group" have been neglected. Secondly, there are hardly any proposals about the development of high-quality relationships. It has been mentioned that these relationships are supportive and therefore have to be favored, but it is seldom said what leaders should do in order to develop high-qualitative exchange relations with their followers. In this regard, Rousseau (1998) points out that LMX theory itself often handles the exchange as a "black box." The complexity of human motivation, the influences of group and organizational effects, as well as the contribution of behaviors, attributions, and evaluations to the development of a particular quality of the exchange are not yet covered by the theory (see among others Mumford et al. 2000; Van Breukelen et al. 2006). Furthermore, the difficulties related to the realization of a win-win situation for all followers of the "in-group" have been neglected. A last critical point that could be raised is that the developmental models of the theory often suggest a deterministic and ideal life cycle without considering feedback loops and unintended developments.

Chapter 7
Idiosyncrasy Credit Model of Leadership

Introduction and Background

The idiosyncrasy credit model of leadership (e.g., Hollander 1958, 1960, 1980, 1992, 1993, 2006, 2008) builds upon the awareness that leadership is an outcome of shared interpersonal perceptions. To become a leader in a given group is the result of an interaction process. This process is market by an assessment of the various contributions of the group members, in which positive (negative) contributions lead to an increased (decreased) level of status of an individual group member (Hollander 1958). The degree of status of a given group member can be compared to a bank balance in the context of this theory (Jacobs 1971). As a consequence, this credit is referred to as idiosyncrasy credit. An idiosyncrasy credit is defined as the "positively disposed impressions" an individual acquires from other group members (Hollander 1958, p. 120, 1960, p. 247). This group-awarded credit allows idiosyncratic behavior to a certain degree before group sanctions are applied (Hollander 1958).

Development of Status

An individual's motivation to belong to a group comes from two sources (see Fig. 1). Firstly, an individual joins a group to satisfy needs that are external to the group (Jacobs 1971). Such needs for example could be the status an academic can obtain from being a member of an association of research fellows. Secondly, belonging to a group is motivated by intrinsic reasons (Jacobs 1971), for example, the participation in a model car club because building model cars is a hobby of the individual. Depending on which kind of motivation is stronger for an individual, the individual joins a particular kind of group.

A group member's behavior is determined by the individual task competence, i.e., the competence to contribute to a group task and its personality. The key

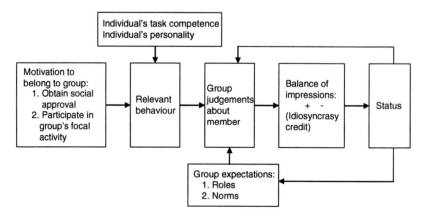

Fig. 1 Development of Status within a Group (adapted from Jacobs, T.O. (1971). Leadership and exchange in formal organizations. Alexandria, VA: Human Resources Research Organization, p. 99, with permission of Human Resources Research Organization (HumRRO))

element of the model is the aspect that group members continuously evaluate the behavior of a single member in order to assess its adequacy. This judgment is basically made on the group members' expectations about adequate behavior. According to the model, members ascribe credit to other members of the group based on their perceived competence, i.e., contributions to the group's main task, and conformity, i.e., keeping existing group norms (Hollander 1993). Competence includes aspects like the control of scarce resources, the access to important information, and the ability to deal with crisis situations (Yukl 2006). Conformity is defined as the members' level of compliance with the existing norms of a group. Literature on idiosyncrasy credit focuses also on other criteria influencing the accumulation of idiosyncrasy credit, for example, intelligence (Hollander 1978), personal characteristics (Kenny and Zaccaro 1983), but also gender (Geis et al. 1985), number of verbal statements (Stein and Heller 1983), and seniority (Insko et al. 1982).

If the performance of a group member is perceived positively by others, and if this member behaves according to group norms, the individual's acceptance rises and the person gains a certain level of status. "Where an individual fails to live up to expectancies, i.e., non-conforms, he (or she) losses credits" (Hollander 1958, p. 120). Eventually, the individual reaches a certain threshold in which the other group members state that it is appropriate for this person to assert influence (Hollander 1960). Consequently, members with a high idiosyncrasy credit are allowed to assume leadership and to influence the group. According to the IC model, leaders of work groups obtain their legitimacy, i.e., the basis for their attainment of the leader status (Hollander 2006), from their so-called high idiosyncrasy credit. A high level of idiosyncrasy credit implies high status within a group and serves as a long-term basis to legitimize leadership. In other words, the accumulation of a high idiosyncrasy credit in the past results in the ascription of leadership and allows the group member to influence others in the future.

Nonconformity of Leaders

If we consider leader behavior we often observe non-conformity. For example, leaders introduce new objectives and tasks or change the member structure. Subsequently, leaders often do not comply with existing group norms in order to introduce innovations. According to the IC model, such behavior should result in a loss of credit and, hence, accorded status. Because of their high idiosyncrasy credit, however, leaders are granted permission to show idiosyncratic behavior before group sanctions are applied. "Once a fund of credits has been accumulated the leader is in a position to be innovative and can depart from normal group practice to a certain degree" (Bryman 1986, p. 8). So, early signs of competence and conformity permit later nonconformity (Hollander 2008).

Moreover, once an individual is assigned to get in the lead, the other group members expect him to show innovative behavior. Being the leader in a group also means to deviate from existing norms to a certain degree in order to take the group forward. Innovative actions, i.e., nonconformity of a leader, must, however, be in line with expectations associated with the leadership role (Hollander 2006). They cannot deviate in any way they want (Hollander 1961). Rather, because they are expected to assume leadership, they are only allowed to act differently in a way that is consistent with their high-status roles (Hollander 1958, 1961). Additionally, nonconformity is related to group success. If leaders deviate from existing group norms to bring in innovations but fail to contribute to the group's main objective, they will be blamed for the failure and, consequently, will lose credit (Alvarez 1968; Hollander 1960).

Elected vs. Appointed Leaders

Hollander and Julian (1970) demonstrate that election and appointment of a group leader evoke different evaluations by followers. As shown, legitimacy of a group leader is the result of a complex process of social interaction. Correspondingly, the ability to influence others differs between leaders who are elected by the group members and leaders who are formally appointed (Yukl 2006; Hughes et al. 1996). Elected leaders have bigger latitude to deviate from existing norms, as they have proven themselves to the group by past performance and conformity (Goldman and Fraas 1965; Hollander and Julian 1970, 1978) and as leader election results in heightened psychological identification between followers and the leader (Hollander 2008). Appointed leaders cannot draw on former performance as they are new to the group. Consequently, their status derives only from the formal position and maybe their reputation based on profession or past positions in other groups. Hence, they are often in a problematic situation because their initial legitimacy is low (Hollander 1993).

Selected Pros and Cons

The IC model, in the first place, enhances our understanding of leadership emergence. It explains how leadership emerges out of the interaction process among group members. Secondly, the model describes how leadership roles, once established, are reproduced and changed. Thus, it allows for process-based studies of leadership. Thirdly, subject to the link between idiosyncrasy credit and leadership, the IC model illustrates why the same behavior by different group members results in diverse effects.

One of the major points of criticism concerning the model addresses the fact that it is (too) rational. By focusing on the categories of "competence" and "conformity" in order to determine the basis of legitimation, for example, emotions are largely neglected (e.g., in the sense of "How well do I get along with somebody?"). Furthermore, political behavior, such as pretending competence in order to get into positions with a high degree of influence, is not considered. That means group members' own interests are neglected by the approach to some extent. Additionally, the process of leadership attribution is not explained sufficiently. Particularly the process of how a collective ascription regarding a person is coming about and the collective acknowledgment of this person as a leader are demonstrated inadequately. Finally, the empirical basis for this approach is considered as being weak since for the most part it is restricted to analyses of small groups in laboratory settings (Yukl 2006).

Chapter 8
Symbolic Leadership

Introduction and Background

The theory of symbolic leadership goes back to ideas of numerous authors (e.g., Pondy 1978; Pfeffer 1981; Smircich and Morgan 1982). Presenting it as a cohesive leadership approach that incorporates various ideas and concepts of symbolic management and leadership and as clearly distinguishable from other theoretical leadership approaches has to be credited to the German leadership scholar Oswald Neuberger (1990, 1995, 2002). According to Neuberger (1995), the approach of symbolic leadership embeds the understanding of leadership reality in a more comprehensive theoretical frame. This frame is based on anthropology (e.g., Geertz 1973), research on corporate culture (e.g., Hofstede 1980; Schein 1985; Sackmann 1991; Martin 1992), and organizational symbolism (e.g., Pondy et al. 1983; Turner 1990; Alvesson and Berg 1992). Additionally, the sociological concepts of symbolic interactionism (e.g., Mead 1934; Blumer 1969) and the constructivist approach (e.g., Hosking et al., 1995) play an important role in this approach.

Symbolic leadership is defined as leadership which refers to, and is based on, the category of meaning. Meaning becomes tangible and therefore can be experienced in the form of symbols (Neuberger 1995). The concept assumes that reality, created and lived by employees in companies, is a social construction, with leadership being a part of this reality (Bartölke 1987). The approach rejects the existence of a level of substantive actions and results, like noted in Pfeffer's (1981a) writings about management as symbolic action. Instead, it is emphasized that the meaningful world of organizations is the outcome of numerous interaction processes creating the organizational reality. Hence, symbolic leadership concentrates on studying values, meaning, interpretation, history, context, as well as other symbolic elements in the leadership process (Kezar et al. 2006).

Meaning is created and maintained through behavior and at the same time influences social behavior. Symbols, as material objects, behavior, or language (Dandridge et al. 1980), carry meaning, or more precisely, a symbol is a particular expression for a number of meanings (Morgan et al. 1983; Neuberger 1990). Leadership takes place within a particular social reality which provides the members of a community with a common preunderstanding and a frame of interpretation. This frame serves as a background to perceive an action as leadership action and to interpret what leadership action is aiming at. Symbols associated with leadership along with other symbols in an organization assist members to define and understand their role within the organizational reality as providing information about status, power, commitment, motivation, and control (Daft 1983).

A Leader's Acting Is Symbolized

Symbolic leadership means, on the one hand, that the leader does not directly influence followers. Leaders and their actions are themselves symbols and, thus, subject to interpretation by followers. In order to result in an appropriate behavior, leaders' actions have to be perceived and interpreted "correctly" by the followers (that means according to the meaning which is intended by the leader). On the other hand, leaders' behavior and leadership substitutes (e.g., organizational structures, systems, and practices as symbols) simultaneously influence the behavior of followers (Neuberger 1995). Consequently, employees are influenced by the actions of leaders as well as by reward systems, organizational principles and rules, work content, practices, etc. (see Fig. 1). To understand organizations and leadership, then, means to realize the various codes members of an organization use to interpret perceived reality and to decode the numerous linkages within complex symbolic systems (Morgan et al. 1983).

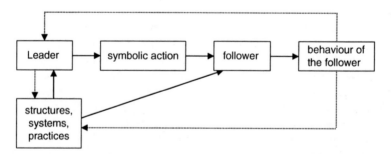

Fig. 1 The process of symbolic leadership (adapted from Neuberger, O. (1995). Führen und Geführt werden [To lead and to be led]. Stuttgart: Ferdinand Enke, p. 252, with permission of Lucius & Lucius)

Leadership as Being Symbolized and Symbolizing

According to Neuberger (1990, 1995, 2002), the concept of symbolic leadership implies two understandings. On the one hand, leadership is conceived as symbolized, that means past leadership behavior resulted in structures, rules, and procedures, as well as organizational practices that are guiding the behavior of followers. On the other hand, leadership is symbolizing, as leaders change meaning of existing aspects of the organizational world or offer meaning for new facts. Both perspectives will be further explained in the following paragraphs.

From the first perspective, leadership is understood as being symbolized. Here, rather the passive and interpretative aspect of symbolic leadership is addressed. According to the framework provided by Morgan et al. (1983), this perspective is more related to the so-called functionalist approaches of organizational symbolism. Every member of an organization as a "system of shared meanings" (Pfeffer 1981a, p. 9) is surrounded by a large number of symbols which have emerged throughout past leadership processes (rules, structures, etc.). Subsequently, leadership is embedded in language, artifacts, and social institutions in order to guide followers' behavior. These symbols appear to be depersonalized because they are perceived as facts (e.g., forms, logos, codified rules, formal structures). They function by providing orientation for appropriate behavior in the organization (Neuberger 1995). Employees are committed to a particular way of behavior which is perceived as obligatory without the leader necessarily being present in person. Consequently, such symbols could be regarded as leadership substitutes and, thus, as given and objectified facts with which behavior is stimulated, guided, and supervised (Neuberger 1995).

In order to ensure influence on the behavior of followers, symbols have to be interpreted in the same way by all members of the group/organization. Symbols are, in a way, storages of meaning which automatically stimulate a deliberate behavior if it is guaranteed that the meaning of a particular symbol is uniformly interpreted by all followers (Neuberger 1995, 2002). Stable orientations and behavior of organizational members is achieved if the same meaning can be deduced again and again from experienced reality in the organization.

The additional point made by Pfeffer (1977), that leaders themselves become symbols, has to be introduced in this regard. If members of an organization attribute causes of observed effects to leaders, then leaders themselves become symbols. According to Pfeffer, the belief of followers in effects of leadership provides a feeling of personal control. In particular, the leader as a symbol provides a target for action when difficulties occur. Moreover, in situations where it is problematic to attribute causality to controllable factors, followers' effort to ascribe causality to the person of the leader and/or the leader's behavior increases. In such situations people more often attribute causes to controllable factors (the leader) in order to retain control in uncertain situations. Pfeffer's perspective, although developed earlier, complements the notion of Neuberger to the effect that leaders themselves are perceived as being symbolized.

From a second perspective, which is according to Morgan et al. (1983) more related to the interpretative approaches of organizational symbolism, leadership is symbolizing. Because facts always have more than one meaning and consequently can be interpreted in different ways, leadership has to ensure that they are interpreted in the intended sense. When interpreting ambiguous symbols, it is the task of the superior to assist with the process of decoding by giving guidance, in order to ensure that everybody understands what has been said and done in a way which results in purposeful follower behavior (Neuberger 1990).

In this second understanding of symbolic leadership, meaning is not deduced from facts but (new) meaning is created through leadership. This sense-making happens, firstly, by deriving new meaning from already existing facts or, secondly, by creating new facts which are provided with sense as well as instructions as to how to interpret them. Following Neuberger (2002), leader intervention means that the leader creates social facts or changes already existing structures, rules, and methods. The effects of these activities, however, cannot be foreseen completely because they are perceived and interpreted differently by different individuals on the basis of their perception and interests. The understanding of leadership as symbolizing therefore means to communicate intended meaning of particular actions toward followers. This aspect has also been highlighted earlier by Pondy (1978), who acknowledged that leadership involves to a large extent symbolic activity. Leaders, who intend a change through their actions, have to reduce the diversity of meanings in order to make a desired effect happen. He claims: "If . . . the leader can put it into words, then the meaning of what the group is doing becomes a social fact" (Pondy 1978, p. 94). So, understanding leadership as symbolizing means to develop a social consensus around labels given to undertaken activities (Pfeffer, 1981). It is, however, not clear whether others will share the provided interpretation. Symbolic leadership is considered to be a process of circulating between symbolized leadership and symbolizing leadership (see Fig. 2).

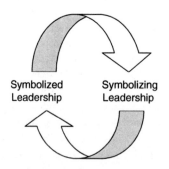

Symbolized Leadership

Leadership **substitutes**: leadership is embedded in routines, techniques, methods, systems, artefacts, etc.

Symbolizing Leadership

Leadership **action**: specific leader behaviour creates or changes reality

Symbolized Leadership   Symbolizing Leadership

Fig. 2 Symbolic leadership as a circulating process (adapted from Neuberger, O. (2002). Führen und führen lassen. Ansätze, Ergebnisse und Kritik der Führungsforschung [To lead and to let lead. Approaches, findings and critique of leadership research]. Stuttgart: Lucius & Lucius, p. 668, with permission of Lucius & Lucius)

Leader behavior or slogans, structures, rules, and regulations are not seen as objective facts but are interpreted by the followers in a process of sense-making. Consequently, meaning cannot be prescribed by the authoritative sender (the leader) but has to be offered, sold, or negotiated again and again to, and together with, the receiver (the follower) (Neuberger 1995). That means leadership emerges as a result of the constructions and actions of both leaders and those being led (Smircich and Morgan 1982). At the same time it becomes clear that there is no choice for a leader to lead symbolically or not, as he/she is always leading symbolically (Neuberger 1990).

Selected Pros and Cons

The approach of symbolic leadership assists to explain leadership reality within the complex organizational world with its manifold interdependencies and apparent contradictions. It acknowledges the existence and influence of culture and construed social reality on leadership and, hence, provides a fruitful framework for leadership research, taking into account cultural and symbolic issues. Highlighting the importance of an organization's social reality and the symbolic interactions of its members, with respect to leadership, provides a background for the meaningful context of, for example, leader emergence, leaders' activities, and subsequent followers' reactions. Particularly, such a perspective conceptualizes leadership as a sense-making process where different understandings of both leaders and followers meet. This process accepts the complexity of the socially construed world in organizations, of which leadership is a part.

Following the ideas of this approach it becomes clear why leaders have difficulties in exerting influence on followers, why they establish formal structures and regulations that are not working, or why followers perceive the leader himself/herself as a symbol. Leadership, in the end, is "realized in the process whereby one or more individuals succeed in attempting to frame and define the reality of others" (Smircich and Morgan 1982, p. 258).

According to Weibler (1995), a critical aspect has to be raised due to the partly rational and instrumental understanding of symbols as leadership instruments. In some cases the leader is presented as "master of meaning" who deliberately creates and uses symbols in order to exert influence on followers' behavior. This quasi-return to the picture of the leader as being able to unilaterally influence followers, however, fundamentally contradicts the subjectivistic and interpretative idea of the approach.

A certain lack of empirical research could be mentioned as being an additional weak point of this approach. There is, of course, a substantial amount of empirical research on organizational symbolism and symbolic management. The leader–follower relation, as socially construed reality, however, has not been fully addressed in empirical studies so far.

Chapter 9
Micro-Politics Approach to Leadership

Introduction and Background

According to the prevailing opinion, the term "organizational policy" can be traced back to Burns (1962), who introduced it into social sciences. He considered political behavior to be the main driver for social changes in organizations. The term "micro-politics" might be defined as the portfolio of those daily tactics with which power is built up and applied in order to extend the room for maneuver and to defy external control (Neuberger 1995). From this perspective, power and politics become essential variables to describe leadership reality in organizations or, as Küpper and Ortmann (1992) put it, organizations are pervaded with politics. Making decisions, formulating rules, creating structures, distributing tasks, or providing instructions are political processes and the people involved are "micro-politicians" or "influencers" as Mintzberg (1983) names them. Consequently, political behavior in organizations is intended to promote or protect the interest of individuals or groups and thereby to threaten the interest of others (Porter et al. 1981). Such behavior is not regarded as being outside the legitimate systems of influence or as being clandestine, as Mintzberg (1983) understands organizational politics. Rather organizational politics and micro-politics behavior – opened and covered – are considered as day-to-day phenomena in organizations and the legitimate system is nothing else but the result of such behavior. Put differently, political processes are considered to be endemic to organizing and organizations (Hosking and Morley 1991). Furthermore, political behavior is not conceived as necessarily dysfunctional but as a matter of fact in organizations and a principal way in which people get things done (Bacharach and Lawler 1998).

Using the framework provided by Gandz and Murray (1980) for classifying the theoretical understandings of political behavior in organizations, politics is conceptualized from a descriptive perspective and means to exert influence and power. Hence, politics in organizations is neither inherently good nor bad, but is a basic feature of organizational life (Ammeter et al. 2002). Organizational politics, and thus processes of micro-politics, are understood as visible results of exercising

I. Winkler, *Contemporary Leadership Theories*, Contributions to Management Science,
DOI 10.1007/978-3-7908-2158-1_9, © Springer-Verlag Berlin Heidelberg 2010

power, or in other words, as power in action (Frost 1987). Subsequently, micro-political behavior is understood as the rule but not the exception. According to the metaphor introduced by Hardy (1993) that "power is a currency and politics represents the method of spending it" (p. 14), the micro-politics approach to leadership clearly emphasizes the spending side.

Politics and Leadership

Understanding leadership from a micro-politics perspective implies abandoning the often unexpressed picture of the rational organization with a pyramid-like, formal hierarchy in which the vertical relationships between supervisors and subordinates are predefined (Neuberger 1995). Additionally, the general understanding is rejected that the goals of the organization govern the activities of organizational members and that there should be some goal compatibility between the leader and followers. The micro-politics approach to leadership processes rather follows the assumption of a polycentric conception of leadership. Every position within an organization is the source and aim of a large number of influences at the same time. "(Everyone) is influencing everyone else in organizations, regardless of job title" (Kipnis et al. 1980, p. 451). Organizations are understood as coalitions in which individuals and groups with varying interests come together and engage in exchanges (Hickson et al. 1981). Consequently, superiors and subordinates also try to satisfy their needs.

The organizational structure or the behavior of organizational members never completely determines the behavior of the single individual since there is always behavioral latitude (Tierney 1996). Hence, leader–follower relations are neither completely determined by the formal hierarchy nor fully defined by individual leader behavior. Instead, there is always room for maneuver that could be (and is) used by both followers and leaders, in order to pursue their own agenda. For example, referring to general managers, Wrapp (1984) demonstrated that in the business world, managers who are deemed to be good keep their goals rather vague and their options open. Instead of behaving as described in management textbooks, they are in fact playing the power game (Wrapp 1984).

According to the ideas of structuration theory (e.g., Giddens 1984), the micro-politics approach to leadership simultaneously addresses the behavioral zone within the structural limits, which are defined by for example organizational structure, and how such limits are created, moved, transgressed or abolished through the micro-political tactics of people involved (Küpper and Ortmann 1992). Members of an organization, no matter whether they occupy a formal supervisor or subordinate position, are hence not determined by structures or rules. They rather deal with structures against the background of their own needs and interests. Although they collaborate, the resulting relationships and structures can change due to shifting interests and/or redistributed resources.

Following Pfeffer (1981b), organizations are understood as political arenas in which independent and purposeful actors (Bacharach and Lawler 1998), i.e., managers

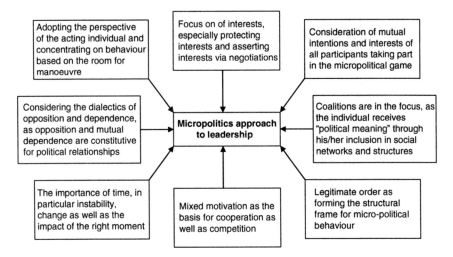

Fig. 1 Aspects describing the micro-politics approach to leadership

and employees, use various micro-political tactics to negotiate structures and rules, to agree on aims, or, in short, to exercise power. In Mintzberg's (1983) terms, organizations are "politicized organizations." They are, however, neither places of disordered political fights nor places in which participants decide purely autonomously. Instead, political behavior takes place within a common frame which is, on the one hand, marked by tradition, biography, and socialization. On the other hand, this frame is formed by values and norms, institutionally secured structures, existing orders, as well as cultural artifacts and practices. The framework serves as reference point for political behavior as it defines (and limits) the range of possible actions and provides the base for interpreting observed micro-political behavior (Mintzberg 1983; Neuberger 1995). To illustrate, in business organizations only certain political actions are possible (e.g., forming coalitions, pooling of resources) whereas, for example, physical power usually is not accepted as a legitimated means of exerting influence. Figure 1 summarizes the aspects describing the micro-politics approach to leadership.

Tactics of Micro-Political Behavior

Literature on organizational politics (e.g., Machiavelli 1984; Falbo 1977; Pfeffer 1978, 1992; Kipnis et al. 1980; Kipnis and Schmidt 1983; Yukl and Falbe 1990; Küpper and Ortmann 1992; Yukl et al. 1993; Neuberger 1995) offers various micro-political tactics which are at the disposal of organizational members to influence others. The following seven dimensions of straightforward and clandestine micro-political techniques aim at providing a general overview:

1. Control of information (e.g., withholding information, designing information systems concerning a privileged use by a few, accumulating specialist knowledge, spreading rumors about others, manipulating information)

2. Control of practices, rules, and norms (e.g., influencing the criteria for control and appraisal, claiming vested rights and common law, defining/limiting the room for behavioral alternatives)
3. Relationship building (e.g., building hidden coalitions, dividing and conquering, establishing friendships by making little presents, establishing privileged relationships)
4. Profiling (impression management, unsettling others, bluffing, performing self-confidence)
5. Control of the situation, establishment of inherent necessity (e.g., making mistakes apparently unintentionally, working to rule, creating fait accompli)
6. Imposition of pressure to effectuate actions (e.g., creating artificial crises and/or making use of actual crises, setting fixed dates, controlling deadlines, postponing meetings, failing to meet target times)
7. Capitalization of chances, timing (e.g., taking advantage of situations, waiting for the best moment, being available, mobile, and flexible).

These dimensions of politics and the related tactics are open to both supervisors and subordinates. Whether and how they are used depends on the kind of organization and the specific context, i.e., the target of political behavior (Yukl and Tracey 2002).

A Model of Political Leader Behavior

In order to enhance the understanding of leadership and processes of social influences in organizations, Ammeter et al. (2002) developed a political approach of leadership. Focusing on the political behavior of leaders, their model highlights various aspects of a so-called "political behavior episode" (Ammeter et al. 2002, p. 755), i.e., the process describing the context, antecedents, tactics, and outcomes of political influence. The model provides an understanding of how a leader's political behavior is embedded in a specific context. Moreover, it aims at highlighting how such behavior is influenced by leader and target characteristics, and how the political behavior of a leader results in (not necessarily negative) consequences for the leader and the target. With their concept, the authors provide one of the few political models of leadership covering relevant aspects like the influence of leader and target attributes on their propensity to political behavior, several kinds of a leader's political behavior, as well as outcomes for both leader and targets. The model has been tested by the authors in later studies (e.g., Douglas and Ammeter 2004). Figure 2 provides an overview of the basic relations between the elements of the model.

Leader political behavior as well as leader and target antecedents are embedded in a specific context. This context comprises five elements: organizational structure, organizational culture, accountability, leader position, and prior episodes. The organizational structure both enables and limits behavioral choices of leaders. Ammeter et al. (2002) clarify this circumstance by referring to the distinction

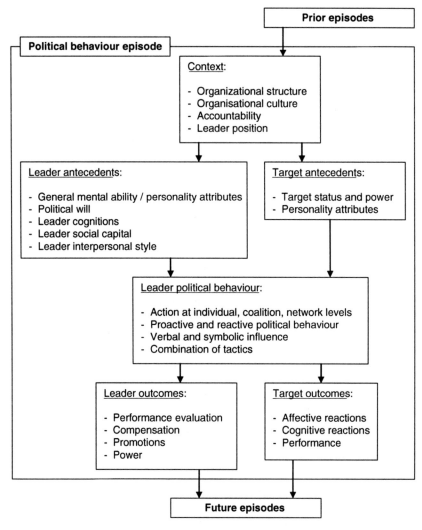

Fig. 2 Political behaviour episode (Reprinted from The Leadership Quarterly, 13/6, Ammeter, A.P., Douglas, C., Gardner, W.L., Hochwarter, W.A., Ferris, G.R., Toward a political theory of leadership, p. 754, Copyright (2002), with permission from Elsevier)

between mechanistic and organic structures introduced by Burns and Stalker (1966). Mechanistic structures are more formalized, feature a clear hierarchy, and emphasize status differences between the hierarchical levels. Hence, the behavioral choices of leaders are closely related to the formal hierarchy and the political behavior of leaders is limited because highly formalized structures limit the free choice of behavioral tactics. In contrast, organic structures provide more room for political action as they are less formalized, feature less emphasis on hierarchical differences, and show low interdependence between single units (see also Porter et al. 1981). Organizational culture as an element of the context is defined as shared values, beliefs, and behavioral norms of an organization. Culture frames and shapes the use of leadership behaviors (Ammeter et al. 2002). In particular, leader behavior must be in line with existing norms and values in order to be accepted. Accountability as a context factor refers to the need to justify decisions to an audience. According to Pfeffer (1981), the main task of managers is to provide reason and meaning for organizational activities. Consequently, the degree of a leader's accountability and hence legitimacy is an important context element influencing his/her propensity as well as the target's attitude toward political behavior (Ammeter et al. 2002). The position of a leader in the formal hierarchy is seen as a context element since it serves as a structural source of power and influence. The position within an organization's hierarchy influences the room or latitude for behavioral choices (Ammeter et al. 2002). For example, top executives usually have more room for idiosyncratic behavior due to their high-level position in an organization's hierarchy. Finally, the history of prior leadership episodes constitutes a relevant aspect of the context. The knowledge of prior leadership episodes serves as a reference point to frame the current episode (Ammeter et al. 2002).

The context influences both the leader and target (or follower) antecedents. These antecedents explain the motivation for leaders as well as the source of their ability to engage in political behavior (Ammeter et al. 2002). At the same time, antecedents of the target describe the followers' readiness to accept and follow the leader's influence through political behavior.

To start with leader antecedents, a leader's general mental ability and personality attributes influence his/her capability and motivation to engage in political behavior. In particular, intelligence and cognitive ability interacting along with personality and social skills influence the capability of skilled political behavior (Ammeter et al. 2002). Self-esteem, Machiavellism, or the need for power are considered relevant personality factors for an individual's motivation to engage in political behavior. Additionally, political will, i.e., the desire and interest in engaging in politics, is considered to be a necessary antecedent contributing to leaders' political behavior. A leader's cognitions, and consequently his/her basic knowledge structures, influence the engagement in political behavior too (Ammeter et al. 2002). For example, the leader's identity shapes the objectives that should be achieved as well as the types of political behavior considered to be appropriate. Furthermore, political tactics deemed as relevant and appropriate are influenced by the leader's beliefs about the power of oneself and the group as well as the power held by other persons or groups (Ammeter et al. 2002). Another antecedent is seen in the social network a leader is embedded in but also the quality of relations to others. This social capital influences the leader's ability to use such social relations as a source for power and influence (Ammeter et al. 2002). Last but not least, the interpersonal style of a leader constitutes a leader antecedent in the model. A leader's social effectiveness, i.e., the ability to effectively read, understand, and control social interactions, along with the political skill, which refers to influencing and controlling others effectively, influences the motivation and ability to engage in political behavior.

Target antecedents that are also influenced by the context are the follower's power and status as well as personality attributes. The relative power and influence of the audience are important determinants of the political approach and the tactics chosen by the leader. In addition, the need of followers to develop a rather close relation to the leader that is positive and supportive as well as the target's trust in the leader that he/she will act in good faith influence the openness of the target for any attempts of the leader to exert influence (Ammeter et al. 2002).

A leader's political behavior that is directly influenced by leader and target antecedents takes place on three levels. Firstly, the individual level consists of political actions directed toward other individuals, e.g., subordinates. Secondly, political action on the coalition level means that a leader builds and uses coalitions in order to combine resources and abilities of coalition members. Thirdly, a leader establishes an extensive interpersonal network in order to gather information and to mobilize support on the network level (Ammeter et al. 2002). On all three levels we can distinguish between proactive and reactive leader behaviors. Proactive leader behaviors cover actions a leader deliberately undertakes in order to influence others and to secure desired outcomes. Reactive political behavior, in turn, should protect the leader's interests and defend positions and resources (Ammeter et al. 2002). Influences itself, regardless of whether proactive or reactive political behavior is considered, could take on verbal as well as symbolic or nonverbal forms of influence. Following the claim of Gardner and Avolio (1998) that the way a leader says something is sometimes more important than what he or she says, Ammeter et al. (2002) point out that, in addition to verbal forms of political behavior, symbolic and nonverbal behaviors by leaders can be powerful forms of influences too. Often, however, leaders combine various tactics. For example, they use open and covered political tactics, engage in various levels of political behavior at the same time, and support verbal tactics with nonverbal or symbolic forms of behavior (Ammeter et al. 2002).

The model describes several consequences of political leader behavior in terms of target and leader outcomes. Target outcomes are among other affective reactions of followers depending on the perceived leader legitimacy and appropriateness of leader behavior. For example, affect-based trust will suffer when a leader's political behavior is perceived as inappropriate (Ammeter et al. 2002). Additionally, cognitive processes influence the targets' interpretation of the situation and the political behavior of the leader. For example, followers' implicit leadership theories shape interpretations of the observed leader behavior. Political behavior that is categorized as typical and effective leader behavior contributes to the acceptance of the leader and his/her actions (Ammeter et al. 2002). Eventually, a leader's political behavior affects follower performance. Ammeter et al. (2002) emphasize that although political behavior can have a negative impact on outcomes of the target performance, the degree of this effect depends on the level of goal congruence between the supervisor and the subordinates.

In addition to the target outcomes, there are several consequences for the leader as a result of his/her engagement in political behavior. For example, influence tactics can affect performance ratings, compensation, as well as promotions.

According to Ammeter et al. (2002), promotions represent a political decision most often made in organizations, and successful political behavior can contribute to personal advancement. Additionally, engaging in political behavior has outcomes for the level of power as well as the access to resources and social networks.

Micro-Politics and the Life Cycle of an Organization

Gray and Ariss (1985) studied different patterns of political behavior in several phases during the development of an organization. Drawing back on their findings, the following Fig. 3 demonstrates that different political tactics are deemed to be effective in various stages of an organization.

In the early phase of an organization, methods of symbolic management (e.g., defining meaning and providing sense) and impression management (e.g., creating an impression, emphasizing individual competence, and communicating/pretending to possess power) are most effective means of political behavior. In the maturation phase, methods to (further) institutionalize already existing power relations are effective as they assist to stabilize inequalities and secure power differences. The potential to exert influence on others is embodied in rules and structures in order to stabilize existing power imbalances over a certain period of time. The last phase addresses changes in an organization. Especially with upcoming changes (e.g., restructuring, redefining organizational objectives), methods of avoiding these changes (e.g., downplay of the necessity to redefine objectives, creating obstacles to change) and, hence, preserving existing power relations are relevant for participants in a powerful position. Here, however, the findings of Gray and Ariss could be advanced by considering the fact that the change of, for example, organizational structures has also implications for less powerful members. For them, employing political methods that particularly aim at supporting changes are useful because existing power structures might change as well. Change for less powerful parties could lead to an enhancement of their power positions.

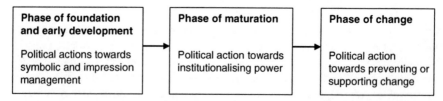

Fig. 3 Political life-cycle of organizations (adapted from Gray, B., & Ariss, S.S. (1985). Politics and strategic change across organizational life cycles. Academy of Management Review 10(4), p. 711. Copyright 1985 by Academy of Management (NY). Reproduced with permission of Academy of Management (NY).)

Micro-Politics Is Not Inherently Bad

Micro-politics is a theoretical approach to leadership that opens up a perspective focusing on the interests of organizational members and the resulting conflicts but also on tactics to enforce rather subjective interests and objectives. This perspective, however, stands in contrast to an idea of leadership implicitly supported by many if not all of the leadership scholars. Leadership should, firstly, contribute to the effectiveness of the individual, the work group, and, subsequently, the organization. Secondly, it should lead to followers' satisfaction. Additionally, the idea of leadership highlights that leaders and followers should act in favor of the company and not (just) follow their self-interests. As a consequence, politics "is still commonly seen as a negative attribute of the organizational environment" (Davis and Gardner 2004, p. 439). Hence, politics is sometimes labeled as "grubby" and understood as – although existing – not accepted behavior. A fear seems to exist that if individuals apply the various tactics offered by the literature, micro-political behavior results in chaos, endless political fights, and ethical misbehavior. According to Neuberger (1995, 2002), however, political behavior is not the sole element of organizational governance. Mintzberg also pointed out that "much more than power determines what an organization does" (Mintzberg 1983, p. 22). That means, micro-politics rather exists and functions parallel to other modes of influence, such as structures and rules, technology, values, philosophies, or strategies. Moreover, micro-politics should never be considered as being independent from the context, boundless, or only dysfunctional.

It seems that the general rejection of political behavior in leadership literature also leads to a negative attitude toward micro-politics as a theoretical approach. This approach, however, neither intends to provide a guideline for effective micro-political behavior nor serves as a manual for the successful enforcement of one's self-interest at the cost of others. Instead, this perspective intends to describe a specific aspect of behavior in organizations which is clearly observable in everyday activity and cannot be reduced to "badly designed structures" (Hosking 1995, p. 57). In short, the micro-politics approach provides explanations for behavior in organizations from the perspective of power and politics – nothing more and nothing less.

Selected Pros and Cons

The micro-political leadership perspective offers manifold possibilities for explaining the interplay between the powerful actors in the everyday life in an organization. This circumstance clearly contributes to the attractiveness of the approach because many of the practices experienced in organizations can be recognized and understood easily. Adopting the perspective of the micro-politics approach to leadership, one can explain why people of equal rank can have various opportunities to exert influence, or why there are even inferiors who have their formal superiors under control.

The abandonment of the understanding of leadership as a unidirectional process of influence and the acceptance of a politically working reality (March, 1962) separates this approach positively from traditional leadership understandings. Furthermore, the widespread view that formal organizational structures and roles fully determine the behavior of their members has been overcome. Instead, this approach draws a picture of leadership as being – at least in part – independent from formal rules and regulations, and influenced by individual interests and political moves. Members of an organization have certain room for maneuver and, thus, freedom. This zone is used by them in terms of following and achieving their own interests and objectives.

A first problematic aspect is the individualistic concept of the approach based upon an understanding of rational members of an organization. They are conceptualized as being able to define their objectives, to analyze the situation, and to choose the appropriate political tactic based on calculated consequences. Such a perspective can hardly explain collective actions, reducing the concept, in the end, to an explanation of achieved aims based on individual behavior. Related to this point, the concept sometimes leaves the impression that people are entirely free in their choice of political actions. This aspect is particularly assessed as dysfunctional (e.g., Morgan 1986), as already mentioned.

A second point of criticism relates to the more or less static presentation of micro-political tactics. Such a description implies that political action finally takes place with just one clever move. The management of power, however, happens over time (Harvey 2006). Political processes in organizations have rather high dynamics as has been shown in early works of, for example, Crozier and Friedberg (1980). This dynamic is as yet only partly addressed by the micro-politics approach.

A third aspect refers to the often implicit assumption that executives are in a powerful position per se. Even if subordinates are regarded as having an influence on the political behavior shown by the manager, e.g., in the model provided by Ammeter et al. (2002), subordinates are still often conceptualized to be in an inferior position. Consequently, understanding subordinates as equal actors in the political arena of an organization and accepting their various ways of actively exerting influence are points that have to be strengthened in this approach.

Chapter 10
Role Theory of Leadership

Introduction and Background

Role theory of leadership as a theoretical approach borrows to a large extent concepts from the sociological role theory and applies these ideas to leader–follower relations. The role concept is regarded as a basic link between the individual and the group, and hence considered an essential element of social systems. Role theory of leadership understands leadership within a group as a result of a process of differentiation by which group members achieve group aims faster and whereby they meet their individual needs. Leadership is considered as being "a part of the problem-solving machinery of groups" (Gibb 1958, p. 103). Based on the different approaches in role theory, the following three basic approaches in role theory of leadership can be distinguished (Neuberger 2002):

- The *structuralistic approach* understands the individual as being permanently influenced by behavioral expectations. The person is typically seen as the focal point of an indefinite number of social relationships (e.g., "father," "superior," and "colleague"). Consequently, the individual forms the focus of behavioral expectations of different role senders, such as other individuals or structures. This context defines particular behavioral requirements which the individual holding a particular role has to fulfill and balance against each other. For example, the head of a department is considered as a focal point of the expectations of followers, of those holding other positions at the same hierarchical level, as well as of superiors from higher levels of the hierarchy. The expectations of these role senders along with the manifold structures and rules of the organization define the behavioral demands of the department head and, thus, determine his or her behavior.

- The *functionalist approach* focuses on the social network the individual is embedded in. From this perspective leadership roles do not exist anymore but only requirements of the system (the organization) which can be met by people holding different positions, regardless of whether they are leaders or followers. For example, it is not important who is involved in fulfilling the task of a department – the head or the members. Actually what matters is that the task is fulfilled. Consequently, the role is defined as a set of functions coexisting with other roles, complementing or replacing them. Accordingly, this approach does not emphasize the particular impact of leader or member roles on meeting objectives. It is acknowledged that formal roles exist; yet, the functionalist approach of role theory only attaches importance to the fact that the demands of the organization are met and not to the specific contributions of superiors or subordinates.

– The third approach, which is assigned *to symbolic interactionism*, understands the behavior of an individual as the outcome of his/her biography as well as the subjective efforts to make sense out of experienced facts and to follow his/her own interests. The roles within a group emerge through interaction, i.e., the roles will be developed and negotiated via active participation of the individual (Seers 1989). Roles, therefore, are neither objective nor externally defined but are always the result of the specific conditions under which they came into being. For example, the role of the head of a department significantly varies across departments within an organization and between organizations. The particular role is the result of an emerging process reflecting the particular context. Of course, certain expectations concerning the behavior of an individual exist. Such expectations emerge with particular positions within specific contexts that are ascribed to individuals. These positional labels (e.g., teacher, daughter, fat man, or husband) serve as indicators for expected behavior (Stryker and Statham 1985). However, besides such expectations what a person is making out of a role depends in particular on the individual himself/herself and is the result of interactions with other individuals. In other words, a "role is itself emergent and inherently incomplete, allowing selves not only to perform, but also to improvise and play with the multiplicity of roles that they encounter in their social and intersubjective experiences" (Simpson and Carroll 2008, p. 43). In contrast to predefined behavioral patterns, this approach focuses on the emergence and dynamic interplay of roles as a result of interactions.

The three approaches are hardly ever found in their "pure" form in leadership research. Although the structuralistic approach is dominant, nowadays it is particularly supplemented and partly replaced by ideas of the symbolic-interactionist perspective. Therefore, in the remainder of the chapter role theory of leadership will be described according to the dominant structuralistic perspective. The developments introduced by scholars following the symbolic-interactionist perspective will also be addressed in order to disclose recent developments of the approach.

Expectations and the Role Set

From a structuralistic perspective the role of a person is described as the total of behavioral expectations which an organization and its members are directing to the holder of a position. That means various role expectations are directed at position

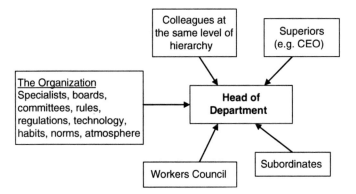

Fig. 1 Example of a role set of a head of department

holders in organizations which can vary according to the role sender. The position of a person in an organization can be determined by individuals as well as by organizational rules, which in turn assign the position to particular functional areas and hierarchical levels. A role is considered to be composed of a number of role segments (see Fig. 1).

As indicated, different individuals and groups address behavioral expectations toward a particular leadership role. Additionally, numerous structures, rules, norms, etc., of an organization serve as role senders as they define expectations for appropriate behavior. It is obvious that these expectations are not necessarily congruent but can be contradictory. It is also noteworthy that besides the role set as a member of an organization an individual is also considered to hold various roles outside the organization. Thus, a manager can at the same time be a father, a member of a model car club, and a member of a political party. Within the structuralistic perspective of role theory of leadership, the behavior of the position holder within the organization is dictated in a kind of screenplay or script. Expectations formulated by others or by the organization determine his/her behavior. Moreover, it is assumed that individuals are not just playing their roles but that the role and their self are congruent.

When changing the perspective and adopting the point of view of the symbolic-interactionist approach, two important differences can be highlighted: firstly, the self as being different from the role, and secondly, the active participation in defining the role by the role holder.

As for the first, people holding a position within an organization are not determined by others' expectations to the extent that these expectations fully determine their self. The role holder is rather being able to differentiate between the role, i.e., referring mainly to the external expectations and the position taken in relation to others (Alvesson 2008), and the self or identity, i.e., referring to an individual's view of himself/herself (Alvesson 2008). Even if self-conception is regarded as contextually fluid (Hogg 2004), i.e., as varying according to situation, the self of a person can in a reflexive way relate itself to the various roles of that

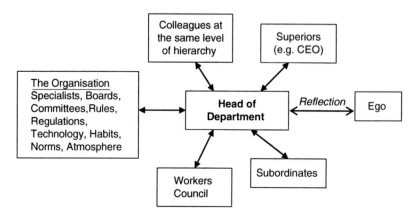

Fig. 2 Role set of a head of department from the symbolic-interactionist perspective

person. A person can recognize himself/herself and consequently his/her roles, and therefore the individual can build up internal expectations regarding his/her own behavior (Stryker and Statham 1985). Hence, an individual is able to recognize his/her various roles in different contexts. Moreover, the individual is able to define the relation between these roles and his/her self and thus differentiate between both. In this respect, a person can literally play a role. Consequently, in Fig. 2, an additional box represents the self of the role holder. The double-headed arrow indicates the reflexive relation between the self and the role.

As for the second, a role holder is not a prisoner in a set of behavioral expectations directed at him. The manifold relationships of a member of an organization are rather the result of the role holder's active participation in the emergence and the content of role expectations. In other words, a role holder is always actively involved in the process of establishing particular expectations about a specific role. As a consequence, it is interactively negotiated as to who is legitimated to claim behavioral expectations and what kinds of expectations are formulated. From this perspective, the manifold organizational structures and rules also are the result of previous human action. They in turn serve as formal guidelines which are perceived differently and, hence, followed by role holders to varying degrees. Subsequently, in Fig. 2, the relations to other organizational members as well as to organizational structures and rules are marked using a double-headed arrow indicating the interactive relationship.

The Process of Role Ascription

Besides the identification and description of the manifold expectations which are directed at a role holder, the process of sending and receiving roles is one main point of interest in role theory. The structuralist approach usually employs the

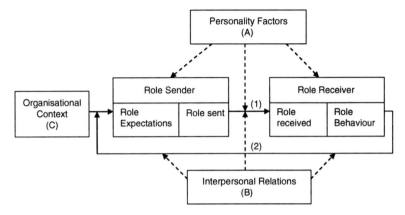

Fig. 3 Role episode (adapted from Katz, D., & Kahn, R.L. (1978). The social psychology of organizations. New York: John Wiley & Sons, p. 196, with permission of John Wiley & Sons Inc.)

so-called role episode according to Katz and Kahn (1978) in order to illustrate these processes (see Fig. 3).

Members of a group have certain expectations regarding the behavior of a holder of a position in an organization (e.g., head of department). These expectations result from the position and the related organizational context, the characteristics of the person, the status associated to that person, as well as from observations regarding past behavior of the position holder. Within group interaction, these expectations are communicated to the role holder (*arrow 1*) with the aim of influencing his/her behavior accordingly. The role receiver recognizes the role message and decodes its content. The reaction of the role receiver regarding the decoded information is labeled as role behavior. *Arrow 2* demonstrates the feedback from the role receiver's behavior to the role sender. This information forms the input to the next role sending sequence. As a consequence, role sending directly refers to previous behavior of the role receiver.

This causal process is influenced by a set of aspects. Firstly, the personality factors (a), i.e., the values, attitudes, and motives, of the sender and the receiver influence the form of sending as well as the receiver's ability to perceive the transmitted information and his/her willingness to meet the communicated expectations. Secondly, the interpersonal relationships between the person functioning as role sender and the one functioning as role receiver (b) have a supportive or hindering effect on the episode. For example, it is assumed that sympathy is accelerating the process, meaning that communicated expectations swiftly result in accordant behavior. The organizational context (c) is regarded as a third influencing factor. Technology, organizational structure and corporate culture as well as, for example, incentive systems particularly influence the expectations of the role sender.

When again changing the perspective and adopting the point of view of the symbolic-interactionist approach, the role episode has to be understood as a symbolic-interpretative process and not as an objective-rational one. In fact, persons enter into interactions with existing conceptions about what other persons – categorized in specific ways – will be like and what they will do. At least in part these conceptions will influence behavior. However, previous conceptions and behavior will likely be modified or changed in the course of interaction (Stryker and Statham 1985). In turn, position holders can also make or develop their roles (Graen 1976). That means they can actively create roles to a certain degree because roles are subject to interpretation and negotiation, and as a consequence exist in varying degrees of concreteness and consistency (Stryker and Statham 1985).

From this point of view, the "sending" of particular role expectations happens by means of symbolic signs, whereas language plays a dominant role as a symbolizing medium. Consequently, the role sender uses a set of symbols (particularly talk and action) in order to communicate behavioral expectations to the holder of a position serving as role receiver. The "sending" of role expectations takes place against the background of cultural experience and rules. This sending has to be interpreted and consequently decoded on this basis. The role receiver, however, cannot directly receive and decode the content of communicated role expectations. In fact he/she needs to learn how this communication has to be interpreted. Consequently, the rules of interpretation for decoding have to be learned as well as sufficient situational knowledge acquired in order to be able to understand the sent message.

The perceived institutionalized context influences the sender's expectations as well as the role receiver's options of behavior. This context, for example, defines which behavior is possible and appropriate. According to Stryker and Statham

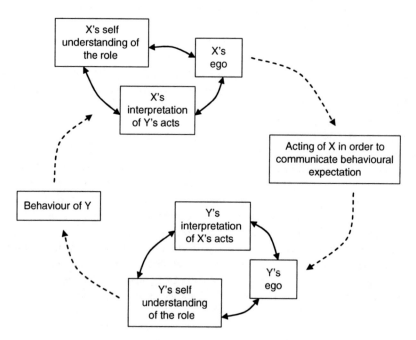

Fig. 4 Schematic role relationships from a symbolic-interactionist perspective

(1985), all social structures impose limits on the possibilities for interaction. Figure 4 outlines the basic elements of the role episode from a symbolic-interactionist perspective using X and Y to indicate the two individuals involved.

On examining Fig. 4 it becomes clear that from the symbolic-interactionist perspective role relationships are shaped more often as a circle rather than as a causal episode with a feedback loop. Additionally, the relationship between roles is embedded in a specific social structure framing (not determining) individuals' perceptions and behavior. The following description of this circle is only to be considered as schematic as the role relationship between X and Y has to be understood as a set of interwoven circles that eventually form some kind of a helix, which leads to a complex picture of the relations between these roles.

To begin with X, this individual defines the situation and classifies it (Stryker 1980). That means X develops a particular understanding of the context, and his/her labeled position and subsequent role, as well as relates his/her self to this role. Based on this understanding (e.g., the self-understanding of being in a role of a follower) X communicates (acts and talks) specific behavioral expectations to Y, for example, perceived as being in the role of a leader. That means X has developed a specific understanding of his/her own role as well as Y's role. This understanding is based on the definition of X's own role (e.g., no interest to take on the responsibility a leader has but interest in having a relaxed job), the organizational context (e.g., Y is the head of the department while X is a member; Y's office is larger than X's; Y has an MBA degree while the other members of the department are skilled workers), as well as former interactions between X and Y (e.g., Y has proven to be an expert; Y is perceived as being charismatic). The acting of X in order to communicate his/her behavioral expectations toward Y, however, is rather seldom an official statement made by X, for instance: "Y, I accept you as the leader, please give advice." In fact, X's actions (e.g., asking Y to solve a particular problem; assisting Y; following Y's orders) have to be understood as symbolic acts that have to be interpreted by Y in order to decode the meaning. This interpretation is influenced by a set of aspects, i.e., the organizational context, Y's self-understanding (e.g., willingness to be an active leader instead of practicing laissez-faire leadership behavior), the relation between Y's self and this self-understanding (e.g., Y is only playing the role as the organizational position ensures high income and status), as well as former interactions between X and Y (e.g., X is always asking Y for advice). Based on the results of the interpretation, i.e., the sense (which is not yet necessarily mirroring X's intentions) Y has made out of X's behavior, Y chooses a particular behavior toward X. This behavior is considered as a reaction to X's communicated expectations and at the same time as a communication of the own role understanding. X interprets Y's behavior, taking into consideration the communicated/perceived expectations as well as the set of impact factors described above. Based on the result of this interpretation X evaluates and possibly alters his/her self-understanding of the own role, the relation between the self and the role, the perceived relation between X and Y, as well as his/her interpretation of the context. Based on these considerations X will choose subsequent acts.

Role Conflicts

Various behavioral expectations are directed toward a role holder in an organization. Furthermore, as is becoming apparent from the description of the approach, the role holder cannot firsthand decode the expectations directed at him/her. These circumstances point to a range of potential conflicts. Following general role theory (e.g., Kahn et al. 1964) it is mainly distinguished between conflicts resulting from different expectations directed toward a role vs. conflicts resulting from being the holder of different roles. Usually, these conflicts are brought forward from scholars following the structuralistic approach using the specific structuralistic tongue.

The intra-sender conflict describes the contradictory expectations a role sender is communicating to the role receiver. This means that, for example, a supervisor is sending expectations to his subordinates to work quickly but accurately and at the same time cost-efficiently. These expectations partly exclude each other and produce a conflict with the receiver as it is impossible for this person to meet all these demands.

The inter-sender conflict addresses tensions resulting from inconsistent expectations communicated by different role senders. For example, a head of department might receive expectations from his/her subordinates in terms of not putting too much pressure on them. Differing from these expectations his/her superiors (e.g., division manager) might express the demand for extra shifts in order to meet annual objectives. Both role senders communicate contradictory expectations, which results in a role conflict with the head of department.

Inter-role conflict means that individuals usually hold a set of roles inside and outside an organization. For example, a head of department is also holding the role of the member of a problem-solving group, the role of a husband, or the role of a member of a political party. Subsequently, the individual is considered to be the focal point of quite different roles with various and partly conflicting expectations.

The so-called role ambiguity addresses the fact that roles and behavioral expectations are defined at various degrees, in terms of concreteness and consistency. Consequently, it is difficult for the role holder to make sense out of the behavioral demands communicated to him/her. This fact could lead to ambiguity regarding appropriate behavior and the role itself.

Introducing ideas from the symbolic-interactionist view the self–role conflict highlights conflicts between the organizational role(s) and the self. Holding a position within an organization involves a set of behavioral expectations directed at the holder, either by other organizational positions or organizational rules and regulations. The position holder, however, is a human being relating his/her self to the role within the organization. As a consequence, the self and the behavioral expectations associated with the position could come into conflict. The problematic relation between an organizational position that demands to be directive and authoritative and a person holding this position but preferring to be more participative could be an example of this kind of conflict.

From a structuralist and functionalist perspective, contradictions between role demands are understood as a kind of temporary instability or as inability of the role holder to balance inconsistent expectations. From a symbolic-interactionist perspective, however, these conflicts are considered as observable outcomes of leadership reality. Subsequently, these circumstances are the apparent result of the inconsistent, multifaceted, and contingent social (dis)order.

Selected Pros and Cons

The ideas of role theory of leadership are supportive in explaining different demands and expectations which are directed at members of an organization as well as the resulting role. It can be shown how specific (leadership) roles in organizations come into being, based on different expectations toward a position holder as well as his/her active concern with these behavioral norms. "(T)he activities of the focal manager and the expectations of the constituencies create a complex social environment in which the dynamic reciprocal influence process develops and continues" (Tsui 1984, p. 31). Role theory of leadership contributes to the understanding of this complexity and dynamic. Additionally, the manifold conflict situations faced by leaders and followers in an organization can be explained taking up this theoretical perspective.

A first problematic point to be considered is the often structuralist and functionalist approach adopted by research on leadership roles. Reducing the behavioral latitude of the individual to the option "whether meeting expectations or not" reflects only to a limited degree the choices members of an organization have. Consequently, Stryker and Statham (1985) speak about an over-socialized conception in this regard, meaning social structures fully determine the behavior of individuals. Here, role theory of leadership should attempt to fruitfully employ concepts that understand norms as rather broad parameters in which individuals make and take roles related to their self and that meet their needs (see for example Turner 1988).

A second problem lies in the highly simplified explanation of the process of the role episode. Only dyadic relationships are observed. But the manifold interactive relationships in organizations usually occur with more than just two people being involved. The process of sending and receiving expectations therefore becomes much more dynamic and complex, a circumstance not yet covered by the theory. Additionally, neither content nor form of the role communication is made the subject of discussion within the role episode, at least in the structuralist and functionalist approach. These aspects, however, influence the perception and interpretation of the role-sending. Eventually, equal size of the boxes in Fig. 3 for role sender and role receiver suggests the same amount of power of the participants. Instead, organizational reality is full of power differences resulting in varying potentials to express and enforce behavioral demands effectively. The symbolic-interactive approach with its particular understanding of the role and role relations highlights interesting perspectives going beyond the rather behavioristic, structuralist, and functionalist approach. However, within research on role theory of leadership this approach is still perceived rather selectively.

Chapter 11
Social Learning Theory of Leadership

Introduction and Background

For a long time motivational and learning approaches to leadership were based on a rather functional understanding of leadership behavior. Focusing on the stimulus-response model, behavior and behavioral change were understood as functions of the consequences a certain kind of behavior might cause. Following the ideas of Skinner's theory of learning (e.g., Skinner 1966, 1969), systematic modification of behavior has to start with the consequences, i.e., rewarding and punishment. In this regard, different possibilities of increasing desired and reducing undesired behavior are at the leader's disposal, in terms of offering rewards to followers or threatening them with punishments. This approach of learning or motivation theory is usually termed as classical and/or behavioristic, and the appropriate stage in the development of leadership theory is named an operant period (e.g., Ashour and Johns 1983). Nowadays, however, this approach is regarded as limited to observable behavior and often criticized by neglecting cognitive aspects. Due to this and other points of criticism, a second, more recent theoretical approach to learning and leadership emerged following the ideas of the social learning theory (e.g., Bandura 1969, 1977a, 1986). This theoretical approach advances traditional ideas of the operant period in leadership theory, focused on the leader as manager of reinforcements (Van Seters and Field 1990). Instead, the role of social and mental aspects in the learning process is considered as well as the interactive and reciprocal nature of cognitive, behavioral and environmental aspects (e.g., Manz and Sims 1980, 1981; Sims and Manz 1982; Luthans and Kreitner 1985; Manz et al. 1987; Luthans 1992, 2008; Sims and Lorenzi 1992; Luthans and Rosenkrantz 1995; Stajkovic and Luthans 1998).

I. Winkler, *Contemporary Leadership Theories*, Contributions to Management Science, 85
DOI 10.1007/978-3-7908-2158-1_11, © Springer-Verlag Berlin Heidelberg 2010

Characteristics of Social Learning in Leadership Relations

The advancement of the behavioral learning theory can be shown at three fundamental differences between operant conditioning and social learning, which in turn
could be considered as fundamental features of the social learning theory. These
differences are the concept of model learning, the role of cognitive processes, as
well as self-reinforcement and self-control.

Model Learning

In contrast to the assumption of operant conditioning which states that learning
takes place through direct enforcement of desired behavior and – at the same time –
suppression of undesired behavior, the social learning theory considers the fact of
indirect learning processes. The concept of model learning describes a learning
process based on observations of the environment, which includes the behavior of
other people. According to Sims and Manz (1982), modeling could be defined as
vicarious learning, which implies learning from the experience of another person
through imitation or participation. Hence, it is not necessary that an individual has
to do all the learning experience by himself/herself, i.e., giving some things a try,
making mistakes, and experiencing the consequences. Instead, it is possible to learn
from observing and copying the behavior of role models (e.g., the leader or
colleagues). Model learning is, according to Sims and Lorenzi (1992), one of the
most important psychological processes by which new behavior patterns are acquired and previous ones are changed. Following Bandura (1969), the authors show
three different kinds of model learning:

– Learning through imitation (learning of new behavior patterns by reproducing
  observed behavior)
– Learning from the consequences of others' behavior (learning of new behavior
  patterns by observing positive and negative consequences experienced by
  others)
– Activation of familiar patterns of behavior (role model behavior activates
  already familiar patterns of behavior)

Considering the ideas of model learning it is possible to explain how people learn
complex behavior patterns, like complex work tasks. Acquiring such patterns of
behavior can be explained more plausibly by defining learning from models as a
form of symbolic representation (Bandura 1969), rather than with explanations
based on reinforcement of discrete behavior by a supervisor. The process of model
learning is characterized by the stages of attention, retention, reproduction, and
motivation (see Fig. 1).

   First of all, the model has to attract *attention*. That means, within the group of
observed individuals one person has to stand out and has to be perceived as a model

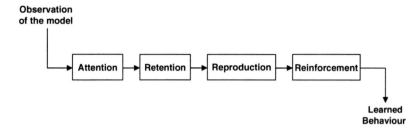

Fig. 1 Process of model learning (adapted from Neuberger, O. (2002). Führen und führen lassen. Ansätze, Ergebnisse und Kritik der Führungsforschung. Stuttgart: Lucius & Lucius, p. 584, with permission of Lucius & Lucius)

on whom attention can be drawn (Bandura 1969). Three variables can either encourage or discourage an observer's attention: (1) the model itself, (2) the modeling display, and (3) the observer (Luthans and Kreitner 1985). It is obvious that individuals having status, prestige, or power – like superiors or valued group members – are more likely to be perceived as models worth being imitated than group-members of low rank. Consequently, the observed behavior of, for example, the group leader or an experienced group member as well as the resulting consequences attract attention of other group members.

In the second stage, the *retention* of modeled behavior takes place. It is necessary that the model, and thus the observed pattern of behavior and the consequences, are memorized. "In order to reproduce social behavior without the continued presence of external modeling cues a person must retain the original observational inputs in some symbolic form" (Bandura 1969, p. 138f.). According to Sims and Lorenzi (1992), this symbolic representation happens through imagination. Individuals remember visually or linguistically the behavior of the model in particular situations.

The third stage, called *reproduction*, describes the physical or mental activities of an observer in order to reproduce memorized behavior (Sims and Lorenzi 1992). It is not enough to simply remember behavioral patterns but it is also necessary to reproduce them through mental or physical imitation. Here it is regarded as important that the observer is sufficiently qualified. "For the modeling process to reach actualization, the observing individual must have the physical and mental capacity to reproduce the modeled behaviors" (Sims and Lorenzi 1992, p. 150). The concept of self-efficacy plays a crucial role in this regard. Self-efficacy (sometimes also called self-confidence or self-competence) generally means to have confidence in one's own ability to manage tasks or situations successfully (Wood and Bandura 1989). Stajkovic and Luthans (1998) show three dimensions of self-efficacy: (1) the level of tasks a person thinks he/she can do, (2) the strength with which this person believes in his/her success, and (3) the general self-confidence of a person. Self-efficacy influences the success of reproduction in such a way that the more a person is convinced that he/she can manage upcoming tasks successfully, the more this person will be involved and persevered in it (e.g., Bandura and Locke 2003).

Fourthly, new patterns of behavior are tested in the final stage called *reinforcement*. If a person assumes that he/she is rewarded for successful behavior by those surrounding him/her, it is more likely that the new behavior will be shown more often than in an environment in which negative sanctions or unfavorable incentive conditions are obtained (Bandura 1969). On account of this circumstance, the motivation stage is often embedded in an environment of tolerating mistakes. Here praise and acknowledgment are rewards for positive (desired) behavior, whereas negative (undesired) behavior is only to a lesser extent or never criticized (Sims and Lorenzi 1992).

The Role of Cognitive Processes

The theory of social learning emphasizes the relevance of cognitive processes within the learning process. As Bandura (1977b, p. 160) states: "Most external influences have an effect on the behavior via mediating cognitive processes. Cognitive processes partly determine which external events are perceived, whether they leave any long-lasting effects, which significance and efficiency they have and how information, which they transmit, has to be used for future behavior." Following the theory of reciprocal interaction, Bandura showed rather early that cognitively developed hypotheses about alternative behavioral patterns and their consequences have the same effect as external stimuli (Bandura 1969). So within the social learning theory, the so far dominating "S(timulus)-R(esponse)-C (onsequences)" scheme of the classical learning theory is extended by the inclusion of the organism (see Fig. 2)

As is obvious from the above-mentioned section about model learning, cognitive processes play an essential role within the learning process. Such cognitive processes mediate the response, i.e., the behavior (Davis and Luthans 1980). The idea of social learning that the external world is interpreted via symbolic cognitive processes is particularly relevant for leadership research, as also leaders and their behavior are part of the external world of the followers. For leaders, however, it is important to consider that the "same" environment is perceived and interpreted differently from each of the group members. For that reason, the picture of one external world does not exist, since each individual imagines his/her own world depending on personal experiences and interests. This world then is specifically perceived and has different meaning for the individual.

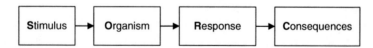

Fig. 2 S-O-R-C schema of social learning theory (adapted from Davis, T.R.V., & Luthans, F. (1980). A social learning approach to organizational behaviour. Academy of Management Review, 5(2), p. 285. Copyright 1980 by Academy of Management (NY). Reproduced with permission of Academy of Management (NY))

Self-reinforcement and Self-control

The third main difference between operant conditioning and social learning is the acknowledgment of self-regulating learning processes of individuals and groups, understood as an addition to external reinforcement. In particular, self-reinforcing behavior and the phenomenon of self-control are considered (Luthans and Kreitner 1985). People and, with regard to leadership, especially followers are able to independently learn complex patterns of behavior.

Self-management is understood as the methods a person can use in order to influence himself/herself (Sims and Lorenzi 1992). "Individuals manage their own behaviors by setting personal standards, by evaluating their performance in terms of these standards, and by self-administering consequences based on their self-evaluations" (Manz and Sims 1980, p. 361). Sims and Lorenzi distinguish between behavioral self-management strategies (strategies to influence behavior) and cognitive self-management strategies (strategies supposed to influence thinking patterns). Strategies to influence behavior include, for example, setting aims independently, self-observation, self-reward, or self-punishment. Strategies to influence thinking patterns contain, for example, positive thinking, mental transformation of obstacles into chances, or imagination of future behavior patterns.

Hence, self-control or self-management describes the ability of individuals to evaluate patterns of behavior by themselves even before external consequences occur. The so-called A-B-C schema (Antecedents-Behavior-Consequences) which dominates the approach of operant conditioning is now further developed into an A-B-E-C schema (see Fig. 3), where "E" stands for self-evaluation.

Individuals – and in the context of leadership, particularly followers – can mentally anticipate consequences of different behavior patterns and, thus, can still evaluate and change their behavior before external and internal (self-imposed) consequences take effect (Luthans and Kreitner 1985; Manz et al. 1987). The processes of reinforcement and supervision are internalized, meaning that followers independently set goals, test and evaluate new patterns of behavior, or solve conflicts. As a consequence, self-management can serve as a substitute for leadership since internal processes function without the presence of a leader (Manz and Sims 1980).

The phenomena of self-reinforcement, self-management, and self-control which can be observed empirically are, however, often used in a normative sense. In other words, highly motivated members of an organization should voluntarily do their best for the organization. Followers are supposed to search independently for new

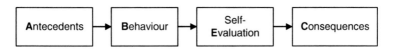

Fig. 3 Self-evaluation as an "additional" part in the control process

and advanced solutions as well as control their activities themselves. For these reasons, the task of leaders is to encourage them to be independent individuals but also to give them room for self-coordination. In short, leaders should enable followers to lead themselves (see, for example, the concept of super leadership by Manz and Sims 1989).

Central Theoretical Model of the Approach

By summarizing the ideas of the social learning theory of leadership, the following theoretical model can be drawn (see Fig. 4). Leader behavior is explained as being reciprocally determined by personal, situational, and behavioral aspects.

The triadic relationship demonstrates that the situation is considered not only as a variable determining behavior but also as the "product" of individual perception as well as of active behavior. Mental conceptualizations of the leader's own personality, objectives, and subsequent behavior influence the reaction(s) of the environment (e.g., followers). The leader's perception of this reaction forms the basis for further interpretations of the situation and the choice of respective behavior patterns. Consequently, the behavior of leaders (and followers) is a reciprocal interaction of personal, situational, and behavioral aspects (Bryman 1992). Hence, neither the behavior of leaders nor that of followers is directly determined. "(T)he leader and the subordinate have a negotiable, interactive relationship and are consciously aware of how they can modify (influence) each others' behavior" (Luthans 1992, p. 287). From the perspective of the social learning theory, a leader is only able to influence others indirectly by providing external stimuli. These stimuli, however, do not directly affect the followers' behavior but are rather selected, interpreted, (re-)organized, and in some cases even transformed by them. Additionally, behavior is regulated not only by external stimuli but also by self-regulatory processes (Pervin 1993).

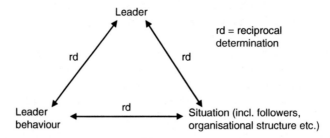

Fig. 4 Central model of social learning theory of leadership (adapted from Luthans, F. (1979). Leadership: A proposal for a social learning theory base and observational and functional analysis techniques to measure leader behaviour. In J.G. Hunt, & L.L. Larson (Eds.), Crosscurrents in Leadership (pp. 201–208). Carbondale, IL: Southern Illinois University Press, p. 205. Copyright 1979 by Southern Illinois University Press. Reproduced with permission of Southern Illinois University Press)

Selected Pros and Cons

On the positive side, the ideas of the social learning theory advanced the theory of operant conditioning, which had been dominating the field of learning processes for a long time. Considering model learning, the social learning theory is able to explain more plausibly the complexity and social embeddedness of the learning process of behavior patterns.

Furthermore, subjective cognitive processes, e.g., perceptions, symbolizations, and interpretations, are incorporated in this approach. Leadership is conceptualized as a mutual process of social learning which contains "reciprocal interaction between behavior and its controlling environment" (Bandura 1969, p. 63). The concepts of self-management and self-control provide a comprehensive basis for leadership training and the development of followers.

On the negative side, it has to be pointed out that the social learning theory of leadership uses a rather simplistic approach of applying its concepts to leadership practice. Although the learning process is described as being full of symbolic representation and interpretation, it is often stated that leaders can learn effective role modeling or can fully understand the specific situation and then apply the appropriate reinforcements.

Additionally, the social learning theory of leadership neglects power structures and politics. A picture of a rather naive world is drawn in which time and resources for external control are unnecessary because organizational members know their own aims and the organization's objectives. Moreover, the members know best in which state they are and what has to be done if a target seems to be missed (Neuberger 1995). However, effects of resistance and politics due to diverging objectives are neglected by the approach.

References

Allen RW, Madison DL, Porter LW, Renmick PA, Mayes BT (1979) Organizational politics. Tactics and characteristics of its actors. Calif Manage Rev 22(1):77–83

Alvarez R (1968) Informal reactions to deviance in simulated work organizations: A laboratory experiment. American Sociological Review 33(6):895–912

Alvesson M (2008) Identity. In: Marturano A, Gosling J (eds) Leadership. The key concepts. Routledge, London, pp 80–83

Alvesson M, Berg PO (1992) Corporate culture and organizational symbolism. Walter de Gruyter, New York

Ammeter AP, Douglas C, Gardner WL, Hochwarter WA, Ferris GR (2002) Toward a political theory of leadership. Leadersh Q 13(6):751–796

Argyris C (1957) Personality and organization. Harper Collins, NewYork

Ashour AS, Johns G (1983) Leader influence through operant principles: a theoretical and methodological framework. Hum Relat 36(7):603–626

Ashkanasy NM (1989) Causal attributions and supervisors' response to subordinate performance. The Green and Mitchell model revisited. J Appl Soc Psychol 19(4):309–330

Ashkanasy NM (1995) Supervisory attributionsand evaluative judgements of subordinate performance. A further test of the Green an Mitchell model. In: Martinko MJ (ed) Attribution theory. An organizational perspective. St. Lucie Press, Delray Beach, FL, pp 211–228

Avolio BJ (2005) Promoting more integrative strategies for leadership theory-building. Am Psychol 62(1):25–33

Avolio BJ, Bass BM (1987) Transformational leadership, charisma, and beyond. In: Hunt JG, Baliga BR, Dachler HP, Schriesheim CA (eds) Emerging leadership vistas. Lexington Books, Lexington, pp 29–50

Avolio BJ, Gardner WL (2005) Authentic leadership development: getting to the root of positive forms of leadership. Leadersh Q 16(3):315–338

Awamleh R, Gardner W (1999) Perceptions of leader charisma and effectiveness: the effects of vision content, delivery, and organizational performance. Leadersh Q 10(3):345–373

Ayman-Nolley S, Ayman R (2005) Children's implicit theory of leadership. In: Schyns B, Meindl JR (eds) Implicit leadership theories – essays and explorations. Information Age Publishing, Greenwich, CT, pp 227–274

Bacharach SB, Lawler EJ (1998) Political alignments in organizations. Contextualization, mobilization, and coordination. In: Kramer RM, Neale MA (eds) Power and influence in organizations. Sage, Thousand Oaks, CA, pp 67–88

Bandura A (1969) Principles of behavior modification. Holt, Rinehart & Winston, New York

Bandura A (1977a) Social learning theory. Prentice Hall, Englewood Cliffs, NJ

Bandura A (1977b) Self-efficacy: toward a unifying theory of behavioral change. Psychol Rev 84(2):191–215

Bandura A (1986) Social foundations of thought and action. A social cognitive theory. Prentice Hall, Englewood Cliffs, NJ

Bandura A, Locke EA (2003) Negative self-efficacy and goal effects revisited. J Appl Psychol 88(1):87–99

Barbuto JE (1997) Taking the charisma out of transformational leadership. J Soc Behav Pers 12(3):689–698

Barling J, Weber T, Kelloway EK (1996) Effects of transformational leadership training and attitudinal and fiscal outcomes: a field experiment. J Appl Psychol 81(6):827–832

Bartölke K (1987) Leadership: nothing but constructing reality by negotiations? In: Hunt JG, Baliga BR, Dachler P, Schriesheim CA (eds) Emerging leadership vistas. Lexington Books, Lexington, pp 151–157

Bass BM (1982) Intensity of relation, dyadic-group considerations, cognitive categorization, and transformational leadership. In: Hunt JG, Sekaran U, Schriesheim CA (eds) Leadership beyond established views. Southern Illinois University Press, Carbondale, IL, pp 142–150

Bass BM (1985) Leadership and performance beyond expectations. Free Press, New York

Bass BM (1990a) Bass & Stogdill's handbook of leadership. Free Press, New York

Bass BM (1990b) From transactional to transformational leadership: learning to share the vision. Organ Dyn 18(3):19–31

Bass BM (1995) Comment: transformational leadership. J Manag Inquiry 4(3):293–298

Bass BM (1998) Transformational leadership: industry, military and educational impact. Lawrence Erlbaum Associates, Mahwah, NJ

Bass BM (1999) Two decades of research and development in transformational leadership. Eur J Work Organ Psychol 8(1):9–32

Bass BM, Avolio BJ (1990) The implications of transactional and transformational leadership for individual, team, and organizational development. In: Pasmore WA, Woodman RW (eds) Research in organizational change and development. JAI Press, Greenwich, CT, pp 231–272

Bass BM, Avolio BJ (1993) Transformational leadership: a response to critiques. In: Chemers M, Ayman R (eds) Leadership theory and research: perspectives and research directions. Academic, San Diego, CA, pp 49–80

Bass BM, Avolio BJ (1994) Introduction. In: Bass BM, Avolio BJ (eds) Improving organizational effectiveness through transformational leadership. Sage, Thousand Oaks, CA, pp 1–9

Bauer T, Green S (1996) Development of leader-member exchange: a longitudinal test. Acad Manage J 39(6):1538–1567

Bennis WG, Nanus B (1985) Leaders: the strategies for taking charge. Harper & Row, New York

Berne E (1961) Transactional analysis in psychotherapy. Grove, New York

Beyer JM (1999) Taming and promoting charisma to change organizations. Leadersh Q 10(2): 307–330

Blau PM (1964) Exchange and power in social life. Wiley, New York

Bligh MC, Schyns B (2007) Leading question: the romance lives on: contemporary issues surrounding the romance of leadership. Leadership 3(3):343–360

Blumer H (1969) Symbolic interactionism: perspective and method. Prentice Hall, Englewood Cliffs, NJ

Boal KB, Bryson JM (1987) Charismatic leadership: a phenomenological and structural approach. In: Hunt JG, Baliga BR, Dachler HP, Schriesheim CA (eds) Emerging leadership vistas. Lexington Books, Lexington, pp 11–28

Brown DJ, Scott KA, Lewis H (2004) Information processing and leadership. In: Antonakis J, Ciancolo AT, Sternberg RJ (eds) The nature of leadership. Sage, Thousand Oaks, CA, pp 125–147

Bryman A (1986) Leadership and organizations. Routledge & Kegan Paul, London

Bryman A (1992) Charisma & leadership in organizations. Sage, London

Bryman A (1996) Leadership in organizations. In: Clegg SR, Hardy C (eds) Handbook of organization studies. Sage, London, pp 276–292

Bryman A (1999) Leadership in organizations. In: Clegg SR, Hardy C, Nord WR (eds) Managing organisations. Current issues. Sage, London, pp 26–42

Burns JM (1978) Leadership. Harper & Row, New York

Burns T (1962) Micropolitics: mechanism of institutional change. Adm Sci Q 6(6):257–281

Burns I, Stalker GM (1966) The management of innovation. Tavistok, London

Calder BJ (1977) An attribution theory of leadership. In: Staw BM, Salancik GR (eds) New directions in organizational behavior. St. Clair Press, Chicago, pp 179–204

Campbell SM, Ward AJ, Sonnenfeld JA, Agle BR (2008) Relational ties that bind: leader–follower relationship dimensions and charismatic attribution. Leadersh Q 19(5):556–568

Chemers MM (1997) An integrative theory of leadership. Lawrence Erlbaum Associates, Mahwah, NJ

Chemers M, Ayman R (1993) Leadership theory and research: perspectives and research directions. Academic, San Diego, CA

Cluley R (2008) The psychoanalytic relationship between leaders and followers. Leadership 4(2):201–212

Conger JA (1989) The charismatic leader: behind the mystique of exceptional leadership. Jossey-Bass, San Francisco, CA

Conger JA (1999) Charismatic and transformational leadership in organizations: an insider's perspective on these developing streams of research. Leadersh Q 10(2):145–170

Conger JA, Kanungo R (1987) Toward a behavioral theory of charismatic leadership in organizational settings. Acad Manage Rev 12(4):637–647

Conger JA, Kanungo R (1988) The charismatic leader. Jossey-Bass, San Francisco, CA

Crozier M, Friedberg E (1980) Actors and systems: the politics of collective action. University of Chicago Press, Chicago

Dachler HP (1988) Constraints on the emergence of new vistas in leadership and management research: an epistemological overview. In: Hunt JG, Baliga BR, Dachler HP, Schriesheim CA (eds) Emerging leadership vistas. Lexington Books, Lexington, pp 261–285

Daft RL (1983) Symbols in organizations: a dual content framework of anlysis. In: Pondy LR, Frost PJ, Morgan G, Dandridge TC (eds) Organizational symbolism. JAI Press, Greenwich, CT, pp 199–206

Dandridge TC, Mitroff I, William FJ (1980) Organizational symbolism: a topic to expand organizational analysis. Acad Manage Rev 5(1):77–82

Dansereau F Jr, Alutto JA, Markham SE, Dumas M (1982) Multiplexed supervision and leadership: an application of within and between analysis. In: Hunt JG, Sekaran U, Schriesheim CA (eds) Leadership beyond established views. Southern Illinois University Press, Carbondale, IL, pp 81–103

Dansereau F, Graen GG, Haga W (1975) A vertical dyad linkage approach to leadership in formal organizations – a longitudinal investigation of the role making process. Organ Behav Hum Perform 13(1):46–78

Davis WD, Gardner WL (2004) Perceptions of politics and organizational cynicism: an attributional and leader–member exchange perspective. Leadersh Q 15(4):439–465

Davis TRV, Luthans F (1980) A social learning approach to organizational behaviour. Acad Manage Rev 5(2):281–290

Den Hartog DN, House RJ, Hanges PJ, Ruiz-Quintanilla SA, Dorfman PW (1999) Culture specific and cross-culturally generalizable implicit leadership theories: are attributes of charismatic/transformational leadership universally endorsed? Leadersh Q 10(2):219–257

Dienesch RM, Liden RC (1986) Leader–Member exchange model of leadership: a critique and further development. Acad Manage Rev 11(3):618–635

Dorian BJ, Dunbar C, Frayn D, Garfinkel PE (2000) Charismatic leadership, boundary issues, and collusion. Am J Psychother 54(2):216–226

Douglas C, Ammeter AP (2004) An examination of leader political skill and its effect on ratings of leader effectiveness. Leadersh Q 15(4):537–550

Duarte NT, Goodson JR, Klich NR (1994) Effects of dyadic quality and duration on performance appraisal. Acad Manage J 37(3):499–521

Duchon D, Green SG, Taber TD (1986) Vertical dyad linkage: a longitudinal assessment of antecedents, measures, and consequences. J Appl Psychol 71(1):56–60

Eden D, Leviatan U (1975) Implicit leadership theory as a determinant of the factor structure underlying supervisory behavior scales. J Appl Psychol 60(6):736–741

Emrich CG (1999) Context effects in leadership perception. Pers Soc Psychol Bull 25(8): 991–1007

Engle EM, Lord RG (1997) Implicit theories, self-schemas, and leader-member exchange. Acad Manage J 40(4):988–1010

Epitropaki O, Martin R (2005) From ideal to real: a longitudinal study of the role of implicit leadership theories on leader-member exchanges and employee outcomes. J Appl Psychol 90(4):659–676

Falbo T (1977) Multidimensional scaling of power strategies. J Pers Soc Psychol 35(8):537–547

Feldman JM (1981) Beyond attribution theory: cognitive processes in performance appraisal. J Appl Psychol 66(2):127–148

Felfe J (2005) Personality and romance of leadership. In: Schyns B, Meindl JR (eds) Implicit leadership theories – essays and explorations. Information Age Publishing, Greenwich, CT, pp 199–225

Fischbein R, Lord RG (2004) Implicit leadership theories. In JM Burns, K Cho, GR Goethals, GJ Sorenson (Eds.), Encyclopedia of Leadership (pp. 700–706). Thousand Oaks, CA: Sage

Freud S (1938) The basic writings of Sigmund Freud. Modern Library, New York Ed. A.A. Brill

Frost PJ (1987) Power, politics and influence. In: Jablin FM, Putnam LL, Roberts KH, Porter LW (eds) Handbook of organizational communication. An interdisciplinary perspective. Sage, Newbury Hill, pp 503–548

Gandz J, Murray VV (1980) The experience or workplace politics. Acad Manage J 23(2):237–251

Gardner WL, Avolio BJ (1998) The charismatic relationship, A dramaturgical perspective. Acad Manage Rev 23(1):32–58

Geertz C (1973) The interpretation of cultures: selected essays. Basic Books, New York

Geis FL, Boston MB, Hoffman N (1985) Sex of authority role models and achievement by men and women: leadership performance and recognition. J Pers Soc Psychol 49(12):636–653

Gerstner CR, Day DV (1997) Meta-analytic review of leader-member exchange theory: correlates and construct issues. J Appl Psychol 82(6):827–844

Gibb CA (1958) An interactional view of the emergence of leadership. Aust J Psychol 10(1): 101–110

Giddens A (1984) The constitution of society. Outline of the theory of structuration. Polity Press, Cambridge, MA

Gingrich, P. (1999) Power, domination, legitimation, and authority. Resource document. University of Regina, Department of Sociology and Social Studies. http://uregina.ca/~gingrich/o12f99.htm. Accessed 25 October 2007

Goethals GR (2004) The psychodynamics of leadership: Freud's insights and their vicissitudes. In: Messick DM, Kramer RM (eds) The psychology of leadership. New perspectives and research. Lawrence Erlbaum Associates, Mahwah, NJ, pp 97–114

Goethals GR, Sorenson G, Burns JM (eds) (2004) Encyclopedia of leadership. Sage, Thousand Oaks, CA

Goldman M, Fraas LA (1965) The effects of leader selection on group performance. Sociometry 28(1):82–88

Graen GB (1976) Role-making processes within complex organizations. In: Dunnette MD (ed) Handbook of industrial and organizational psychology. Rand McNally, Chicago, pp 1202–1245

Graen GB, Cashman J (1975) A role making model on formal organizations: a developmental approach. In: Hunt JG, Larson LL (eds) Leadership frontiers. Kent State University Press, Kent, OH, pp 143–165

Graen GB, Scandura TA (1987) Toward a psychology of dyadic organizing. In: Cummings TG, Staw BM (eds) Research in organizational behaviour. Free Press, Greenwich, CT, pp 175–208

Graen GB, Uhl-Bien M (1991) The transformation of professionals into self-managing and partially self-designing contributions: toward a theory of leader making. J Manage Syst 3(3):33–48

Graen GB, Uhl-Bien M (1995) Relationship-based approach to leadership: development of leader-member exchange (LMX) theory of leadership over 25 years: applying a multi-level multi-domain perspective. Leadersh Q 6(2):219–247

Graen GB, Wakabayashi M, Graen MR, Graen MG (1990) International generalizability of American hypothesis about Japanese management progress: a strong inference investigation. Leadersh Q 1(1):1–11

Gray B, Ariss SS (1985) Politics and strategic change across organizational life cycles. Acad Manage Rev 10(4):707–723

Green SG, Anderson SE, Shivers SL (1996) Demographic and organizational influences on leader-member exchange and related work attitudes. Organ Behav Hum Decis Process 66(2):203–214

Green SG, Mitchell TR (1979) Attributional processes of leaders in leader-member interactions. Organ Behav Hum Perform 23(3):429–458

Grint K (ed) (1997) Leadership. Oxford University Press, Oxford

Hardy C (1993) What do we really mean by power an politics? A review of the literature. In: Dlugos G, Dorow W, Farrell D (eds) Organizational politics. From conflict-suppression to rational conflict-management. Gabler, Wiesbaden, pp 1–26

Harris TA (1967) I'm OK-You're OK. Harper & Row, New York

Harvey M (2006) Leadership and the human condition. In: Goethals GR, Sorenson GLJ (eds) The quest for a general theory of leadership. Edward Elgar, Cheltenham, pp 39–45

Heider F (1958) The psychology of interpersonal relations. Wiley, New York

Heller FA (2002) Leadership. In: Sorge A (ed) Organization. Thompson Learning, London, pp 388–401

Henderson DJ, Wayne SJ, Bommer WH, Shore LM, Tetrick LE (2008) Leader-member exchange, differentiation, and psychological contract fulfillment: a multilevel examination. J Appl Psychol 93(6):1208–1219

Hickson DJ, Astley WG, Butler RJ, Wilson DC (1981) Organization as power. In: Cummings TG, Staw BM (eds) Research in organizational behaviour. JAI-Press, Greenwich, CT, pp 151–196

Hofstede G (1980) Culture's consequences: international differences in work-related values. Sage, Beverly Hills

Hogg MA (2004) Social identity and leadership. In: Messick DM, Kramer RM (eds) The psychology of leadership. New perspectives and research. Lawrence Erlbaum Associates, Mahwah, NJ, pp 53–80

Hollander EP (1958) Conformity, status, and idiosyncrasy credit. Psychol Rev 65(2):117–127

Hollander EP (1960) Competence and conformity in the acceptance of influence. J Abnorm Soc Psychol 61(3):361–365

Hollander EP (1961) Some effects of perceived status on response to innovative behavior. Journal of Abnormal and Social Psychology 63(2):247–250

Hollander EP (1978) Leadership dynamics: a practical guide to effective relationships. Macmillan, New York

Hollander EP (1980) Leadership and social exchange processes. In: Gergen KJ, Greenberg MS, Willis RH (eds) Social exchange: advances in theory and research. Plenum, New York, pp 103–118

Hollander EP (1992) The essential interdependence of leadership and followership. Curr Dir Psychol Sci 1(2):71–75

Hollander EP (1993) Legitimacy, power, and influence. In: Chemers M, Ayman R (eds) Leadership theory and research: perspectives and research directions. Academic, San Diego, CA, pp 29–48

Hollander EP (2006) Influence processes in leadership-followership. Inclusion and the idiosyncrasy credit model. In: Hantula D (ed) Advances in social and organizational psychology. A tribute to Ralph Rosnow. Erlbaum, Mahawa, NJ, pp 293–314

Hollander EP (2008) Inclusive leadership. The essential leader-follower relationship. Routledge, New York

Hollander EP, Julian JW (1970) Studies in leader legitimacy, influence, and innovation. In: Berkowitz LL (ed) Advances in experimental social psychology. Academic, New York, pp 33–69

Hollander EP, Julian JW (1978) A further look at leader legitimacy, influence, and innovation. In: Berkowitz LL (ed) Group processes. Academic, New York, pp 153–165

Homans GC (1958) Social behavior as exchange. Am J Sociol 63:597–606

Hosking DM (1995) Constructing power. Entitative and relational approaches. In: Hosking DM, Dachler HP, Gergen KJ (eds) Management and organization. Relational alternatives to individualism. Ashgate, Vermont, pp 51–70

Hosking DM, Dachler HP, Gergen KJ (1995) Management and organization: relational alternatives to individualism. Ashgate, Vermont

Hosking DM, Morley IE (1991) A social psychology of organizing. Harvester Wheatsheaf, New York

House RJ (1977) A 1976 theory of charismatic leadership. In: Hunt JG, Larson LL (eds) Leadership: the cutting edge. Southern Illinois University Press, Carbondale, IL, pp 189–205

House RJ (1999) Weber and the neo-charismatic leadership paradigm: a response to Beyer. Leadersh Q 10(4):563–575

House RJ, Delbecq A, Taris TW (1998) Value based leadership: an integrated theory and an empirical test. Unpublished manuscript, University of Pennsylvania

House RJ, Hanges PJ (2004) Research design. In: House RJ, Hanges PJ, Javidan M, Dorfman PW, Gupta V (eds) Culture, leadership, and organizations: the GLOBE study of 62 societies. Sage, Thousand Oaks, CA, pp 95–101

House RJ, Hanges PJ, Ruiz-Quintanilla SA, Dorfman PW, Javidan M, Dickson MW, Gupta V, GLOBE (1999) Cultural influences on leadership and organizations: project GLOBE. In: Mobley WH, Gessner MJ, Arnold V (eds) Advances in global leadership. JAI-Press, Stamford, CN, pp 171–233

House RJ, Hanges PJ, Javidan M, Dorfman PW, Gupta V (2004) Culture, leadership, and organizations: the GLOBE study of 62 societies. Sage, Thousand Oaks, CA

House RJ, Javidan M (2004) Overview of GLOBE. In: House RJ, Hanges PJ, Javidan M, Dorfman PW, Gupta V (eds) Culture, leadership, and organizations: the GLOBE study of 62 societies. Sage, Thousand Oaks, CA, pp 9–28

House RJ, Shamir B (1993) Toward the integration of transformational, charismatic and visionary theories of leadership. In: Chemers M, Ayman R (eds) Leadership theory and research: perspectives and research directions. Academic, San Diego, CA, pp 81–108

House RJ, Shamir B (1995) Führungstheorien – Charismatische Führung [Leadership theories – Charismatic leadership]. In: Kieser A, Reber G, Wunderer R (eds) Handwörterbuch der Führung. C.E. Poeschel, Stuttgart, pp 878–897

Howell JM, Avolio BJ (1993) Transformational leadership, transactional leadership, locus of control and support for innovation: key predictors of consolidated-business-unit performance. J Appl Psychol 78(6):891–902

Howell JM, Shamir B (2005) The role of followers in the charismatic leadership process: Relationships and their consequences. Academy of Management Review 30(1):96–112

Hoyt CL (2008) Leader-Follower relations. In: Marturano A, Gosling J (eds) Leadership. The key concepts. Routledge, London, pp 90–94

Huang X, Wright RP, Chiu WCK, Wang C (2008) Relational schemas as sources of evaluation and misevaluation of leader–member exchanges: some initial evidence. Leadersh Q 19(3):266–282

Hughes RL, Ginnett RC, Curphy GJ (1996) Leadership. Enhancing the lessons of experience. Irwin, Chicago

Hunt JG (1984) Managerial behaviour from a "radical" perspective. In: Hunt JG, Hosking D, Schriesheim CA, Steward R (eds) Leaders and managers: International perspectives on managerial behavior and leadership. Pergamon Press, New York, pp 275–277

Hunt JG (1991) Leadership: a new synthesis. Sage, New York

Hunt JG, Baliga BR, Dachler HP, Schriesheim CA (1987) Emerging leadership vistas. Lexington Books, Lexington

Hunt JG, Boal KB, Dodge GE (1999) The effects of visionary and crisis-responsive charisma on followers: an exerimental examination of two kinds of charismatic leadership. Leadersh Q 10(3):423–448

Insko CA, Gilmore R, Moehle D, Lipsitz A, Drenan S, Thibaut JW (1982) Seniority in the generational transition of laboratory groups: the effects of social familiarity and task experience. J Exp Soc Psychol 18(6):557–580

Jacobs TO (1971) Leadership and exchange in formal organizations. Human Resources Research Organization, Alexandria, VA

Jones EE, Davis KE (1965) From acts to dispositions. In: Berkowitz L (ed) Advances in experimental social psychology. Academic, New York, pp 219–266

Jones EE, Nisbett RE (1987) The actor and the observer: divergent perceptions of the causes of behaviour. In: Jones EE, Kanouse DE, Kelley HH, Nisbett RE, Valins S, Weiner B (eds) Attribution: perceiving the causes of behavior. Lawrence Erlbaum Associates, Hillsdale, NJ, pp 79–94

Jordan DJ (1998) Leadership: the state of the research. Parks Recreation 33(10):32–40

Kahn RL, Wolfe DM, Quinn RP, Rosenthal RA, Snoek JD (1964) Organizational stress: studies in role conflict and amibuity. Wiley, New York

Katz D, Kahn RL (1966) The social psychology of organizations. Wiley, New York

Katz D, Kahn RL (1978) The social psychology of organizations. New York: John Wiley & Sons

Keller T (1999) Images of the familiar: individual differences and implicit leadership theories. Leadersh Q 10(4):589–606

Kelley HH (1967) Attribution theory in social psychology. In: Levine D (ed) Nebraska symposium on motivation. University of Nebraska Press, Lincoln, pp 192–238

Kelley HH (1971) Attribution in social interaction. General Learning Press, Morristown, NJ

Kelley HH (1972) Causal schemata and the attribution process. In: Jones E, Kanouse D, Kelley H, Nisbett R, Valins S, Weiner B (eds) Attribution: perceiving causes of behavior. General Learning Press, Morristown, pp 151–176

Kelley HH (1973) The process of causal attribution. Am Psychol 28(2):107–128

Kenney RA, Blascovich J, Shaver PR (1994) Implicit leadership theories for new leaders. Basic Appl Soc Psychol 15(4):409–437

Kenny DA, Zaccaro SJ (1983) An estimate of variance due to traits in leadership. J Appl Psychol 68(4):678–685

Kets deVries MFR (1988) Prisoners of leadership. Hum Relat 41(3):261–280

Kets de Vries MFR (1989) Prisoners of leadership. Wiley, New York

Kets de Vries MFR (1997) The leadership mystique. In: Grint K (ed) Leadership. classical, contemporary, and critical approaches. Oxford University Press, Oxford, pp 250–271

Kets de Vries MFR (2004) Organizations on the couch: a clinical perspective on organizational dynamics. Eur Manage J 22(2):183–200

KetsdeVries MFR, Miller D (1984) The neurotic organization. Diagnosing and changing counterproductive styles of management. San Francisco, CA, Jossey-Bass

Kezar AJ, Carducci R, Contreras-McGavin M (2006) Rethinking the "L" word in higher education: the revolution in research on leadership. Jossey-Bass, San Francisco, CA

Kipnis D, Schmidt SM (1983) An influence perspective on bargaining within organizations. In: Bazerman M, Lewicki R (eds) Negotiating in organizations. Sage, Beverly Hills, pp 303–319

Kipnis D, Schmidt SM, Wilkinson I (1980) Intraorganizational influence tactics: explorations in getting one's way. J Appl Psychol 65(4):440–452

Kirkbride P (2006) Developing transformational leaders: the full range leadership model in action. Ind Commer Train 38(1):23–32

Kirkpatrick SA, Locke EA (1996) Direct and indirect effects of three core charismatic leadership components on performance and attitudes. J Appl Psychol 81(1):36–51

Klein KJ, House RJ (1995) On fire: charismatic leadership and levels of analysis. Leadersh Q 6(2):183–198

Knowlton WA, Mitchell TR (1980) Effects of causal attribution on a supervisors' evaluation of subordinate performance. J Appl Psychol 65(4):459–566

Konrad E (2000) Implicit leadership theories in Eastern and Western Europe. Soc Sci Inform 39(2):335–347

Kraus G, Gemmill G (1990) Idiosyncratic effects of implicit theories of leadership. Psychol Rep 66(1):247–257

Küpper W, Ortmann G (1992) Mikropolitik: rationalität, macht und spiele in organisationen [Micropolicy: rationality, power and games in organizations]. Westdeutscher Verlag, Opladen

Lewin K, Lippitt R, White RK (1939) Patterns of aggressive behavior in experimentally created "social climates". J Soc Psychol 10(2):271–299

Liden RC, Graen GB (1980) Generalizability of the vertical dyad linkage model of leadership. Acad Manage J 23(3):451–465

Liden RC, Maslyn JM (1998) Multidimensionality of leader-member exchange: an empirical assessment through scale development. J Manage 24(1):43–50

Liden RC, Wayne SJ, Stilwell D (1993) A longitudinal study on the early development of leader-member exchange. J Appl Psychol 78(4):662–674

Lord RG (1985) An information processing approach to social perceptions, leadership and behavioral measurement in organizations. In: Cummings TG, Staw BM (eds) Research in organizational behaviour. JAI-Press, Greenwich, CT, pp 87–128

Lord RG, Foti RJ (1986) Schema theories, information processing, and organizational behavior. In: Sims HP Jr, Gioia DA (eds) The thinking organization. Dynamics of organizational social cognition. Jossey-Bass, San Francisco, CA, pp 20–48

Lord RG, Foti RJ, DeVader C (1984) A test of leadership categorization theory: internal structure, information processing, and leadership perceptions. Organ Behav Hum Perform 34(3): 343–378

Lord RG, Foti RJ, Phillips JS (1982) A theory of leadership categorization. In: Hunt JG, Sekaran U, Schriesheim CA (eds) Leadership beyond established views. Southern Illinois University Press, Carbondale, IL, pp 104–121

Lord RG, Maher KJ (1990) Perceptions of leadership and their implications in organizations. In: Carroll JS (ed) Applied social psychology and organizational settings. Lawrence Erlbaum Associates, Hillsdale, NJ, pp 129–154

Lord RG, Maher KJ (1993) Leadership and information processing: linking perceptions to performance. Routledge, London

Lord RG, Smith JE (1983) Theoretical, informational, information processing, and situational factor affecting attributional theories of organizational behavior. Acad Manage Rev 8(1): 50–60

Luthans F (1979) Leadership: a proposal for a social learning theory base and observational and functional analysis techniques to measure leader behaviour. In: Hunt JG, Larson LL (eds) Crosscurrents in leadership. Southern Illinois University Press, Carbondale, IL, pp 201–208

Luthans F (1992) Organizational behavior. McGraw-Hill, New York

Luthans F (2008) Organizational behaviour. McGraw-Hill, New York

Luthans F, Hodgetts RM, Rosenkrantz SA (1988) Real managers. Ballinger, Cambridge, MA

Luthans F, Kreitner R (1985) Organizational behavior modification and beyond. An operant and social learning approach. Scott, Foresman and Company, Glenview, IL

Maccoby M (1977) The gamesman: the new corporate leaders. Simon & Schuster, New York

Maccoby M (2000) Narcissistic leaders. Harv Bus Rev 78(1):68–77

Machiavelli N (1984) The prince. Bantam Classics, New York Reissue edition

Maher KJ (1997) Gender-related stereotypes of transformational and transactional leadership. Sex Roles 37(3/4):209–225

Manz CC, Mossholder KW, Luthans F (1987) An integrated perspective of self-control in organizations. Adm Soc 19(1):3–24

Manz CC, Sims HP (1980) Self-management as a substitute for leadership: a social learning perspective. Acad Manage Rev 5(3):361–367

Manz CC, Sims HP (1981) Vicarious learning: the influence of modeling on organizational behavior. Acad Manage Rev 6(1):105–113

Manz CC, Sims HP (1989) SuperLeadership: leading others to lead themselves. Prentice Hall, New York

March JG (1962) The business firm as a political coalition. J Polit 24(4):662–678

Martin J (1992) Cultures in organizations: three perspectives. Oxford University Press, New York

Marion R, Uhl-Bien M (2001) Leadership in complex organizations. Leadersh Q 12(4):389–418

Martinko MJ, Gardner WL (1982) Learned helplessness: an alternative explanation for performance deficits. Acad Manage Rev 7(2):413–417

Martinko MJ, Gardner WL (1987) The leader/member attribution process. Acad Manage Rev 12(2):235–249

Martinko MJ, Harvey P, Douglas SC (2007) The role, function, and contobution of attribution theory to leadership. A review. Leadersh Q 18(6):561–585

McElroy JC (1982) A typology of attribution leadership research. Acad Manage Rev 7(3):413–417

McElroy JC, Hunger JD (1987) Leadership theory as causal attributions of performance. In: Hunt JG, Baliga BR, Dachler HP, Schriesheim CA (eds) Emerging leadership vistas. Lexington Books, Lexington, pp 169–182

Mead GH (1934) Mind, self and society. University of Chicago Press, Chicago

Medvedeff ME, Lord RG (2006) Implicit leadership theories as dynamic processing structures. In: Shamir B, Pillai R, Bligh MC, Uhl-Bien M (eds) Follower-centered perspectives on leadership: a tribute to the memory of James R. Meindl. Information Age Publishing, Charlotte, NC, pp 19–50

Meindl JR (1990) On leadership: an alternative to the conventional wisdom. In: Cummings TG, Staw BM (eds) Research in organizational behaviour. JAI Press, Greenwich, CT, pp 159–203

Meindl JR, Ehrlich SB, Dukerich JM (1985) The romance of leadership. Adm Sci Q 30(1):78–102

Messick DM (2004) On the psychological exchange between leaders and followers. In: Messick DM, Kramer RM (eds) The psychology of leadership. New perspectives and research. Lawrence Erlbaum Associates, Mahwah, NJ, pp 81–96

Mintzberg H (1983) Power in and around organizations. Prentice Hall, Englewood Cliffs, NJ

Mitchell TR, Green SB, Wood RE (1981) An attributional model of leadership and the poor performing subordinate. Development and validation. In: Cummings TG, Staw BM (eds) Research in organizational behaviour. JAI-Press, Greenwich, CT, pp 197–234

Mitchell TR, Wood RE (1980) Supervisors' responses to subordinate poor performance. A test of an attributional model. Organ Behav Hum Perform 25(1):123–138

Morgan G (1986) Images of organization. Sage, Newbury Park

Morgan G, Frost PJ, Pondy LR (1983) Organizational symbolism. In: Pondy LR, Frost PJ, Morgan G, Dandridge TC (eds) Organizational symbolism. JAI Press, Greenwich, CT, pp 3–38

Müller A, Schyns B (2005) The perception of leadership – leadership as perception: an exploration using the repertory grid-technique. In: Schyns B, Meindl JR (eds) Implicit leadership theories – essays and explorations. Information Age Publishing, Greenwich, CT, pp 81–101

Mullins LJ (2007) Management and organizational behaviour. Prentice Hall, Harlow

Mumford MD, Dansereau F, Yammarino FJ (2000) Followers, motivations, and levels of analysis: the case of individualized leadership. Leadersh Q 11(2):313–341

Nahrgang JD, Morgeson FP, Ilies R (2009) The development of leader–member exchanges: exploring how personality and performance influence leader and member relationships over time. Organ Behav Hum Decis Process 108(2):256–266

Neuberger O (1990) Führung (ist) symbolisiert. Plädoyer für eine sinnvolle Führungsforschung [Leadership is symbolized (symbolizes). Plea for meaningful leadership research]. In:

Wiendieck G, Wiswede G (eds) Führung im Wandel. Neue Perspektiven für Führungs-
   forschung und Führungspraxis. Ferdinand Enke, Stuttgart, pp 89–130
Neuberger O (1995) Führen und Geführt werden [To lead and to be led]. Ferdinand Enke, Stuttgart
Neuberger O (1999) Mikropolitik [Micro-Politics]. In: von Rosenstiel L, Regnet E, Domsch ME
   (eds) Führung von Mitarbeitern. Handbuch für erfolgreiches Personalmanagement. Schäffer
   Poeschel, Stuttgart, pp 39–46
Neuberger O (2002) Führen und führen lassen. Ansätze, Ergebnisse und Kritik der Führungs-
   forschung [To lead and to let lead. Approaches, findings and critique of leadership research].
   Lucius & Lucius, Stuttgart
Northouse PG (1997) Leadership. Theory and practice. Sage, Thousand Oaks, CA
Northouse PG (2004) Leadership. Theory and practice. Sage, Thousand Oaks, CA
Northouse PG (2007) Leadership. Theory and practice. Sage, Thousand Oaks, CA
Offermann LR, Kennedy JK Jr, Wirtz PW (1994) Implicit leadership theories – Content, structure
   and generalizability. Leadersh Q 50(1):31–41
Ogden TH (1979) On projective indentification. Int J Psychoanal 60(3):357–373
Ogden T (1986) The matrix of the mind. Object relations theory and the psychoanalytic dialogue.
   Jason Aronson, Northwale, NJ
Pervin LA (1993) Personality. Theory and research. Wiley, New York
Pfeffer J (1977) The ambiguity of leadership. Acad Manage Rev 2(1):104–112
Pfeffer J (1978) The micropolitics of organizations. In: Meyer MW (ed) Environments and
   organizations. Jossey-Bass, San Francisco, CA, pp 29–50
Pfeffer J (1981a) Management as symbolic action: the creation and maintenance of organizational
   paradigms. In: Cummings TG, Staw BM (eds) Research in organizational behaviour. JAI-
   Press, Greenwich, CT, pp 1–52
Pfeffer J (1981b) Power in organizations. Pitman, Marshfield, MA
Pfeffer J (1992) Managing with power: politics and influence in organizations. Harvard Business
   School Press, Watertown
Pillai R (1996) Crisis and the emergence of charismatic leadership in groups: an experimental
   investigation. J Appl Soc Psychol 26(6):543–562
Podsakoff PM, Bommer WH, Podsakoff NP, MacKenzie SB (2006) Relationships between
   leader reward and punishment behavior and subordinate attitudes, perceptions, and behaviors:
   a meta-analytic review of existing and new research. Organ Behav Hum Decis Process
   99(2):113–142
Pondy LR (1978) Leadership is a language game. In: McGall MW Jr, Lombardo MM (eds)
   Leadership: where else can we go? Duke University Press, Durham, pp 87–99
Pondy LR, Frost PJ, Morgan G, Dandridge TC (eds) (1983) Organizational symbolism. JAI-Press,
   Greenwich, CT
Porter LW, Allen RW, Angle HL (1981) The politics of upward influence in organizations. In:
   Cummings TG, Staw BM (eds) Research in organizational behaviour. JAI-Press, Greenwich,
   CT, pp 109–149
Ritzer G (2007) Sociological theory, 7th edn. McGraw-Hill, New York
Ropo A, Hunt JG (1999) Leadership and organizational change: some findings from a processual
   grounded theory study. In: Wagner JA III (ed) Advances in qualitative research. JAI-Press,
   Stamford, CT, pp 169–200
Rost JC (1991) Leadership for the twenty-first century. Praeger, Westport, CT
Rousseau DM (1998) LMX meets the psychological contract: looking inside the black box of
   leader-member exchange. In: Dansereau F, Yammarino FJ (eds) Leadership: the multiple-level
   approaches. Contemporary and alternative. JAI-Press, Stamford, CT, pp 149–154
Sackmann SA (1991) Cultural knowledge in organizations: exploring the collective mind. Sage,
   Newbury Park
Sankowsky D (1995) The charismatic leader as narcissist: understanding the abuse of power.
   Organ Dyn 23(4):57–71
Schein EH (1985) Organizational culture and leadership. Jossey-Bass, San Francisco, CA

Schyns B, Croon MA (2006) A model of task demands, social structure, and leader-member exchange and their relationship to job satisfaction. Int J Hum Res Manage 17(4):602–615

Schyns B, Meindl JR (2005) An overview of implicit leadership theories and their application in organization practice. In: Schyns B, Meindl JR (eds) Implicit leadership theories – essays and explorations. Information Age Publishing, Greenwich, CT, pp 15–36

Schyns B, Kroon B, Moors G (2008) Follower characteristics and the perception of leader-member exchange. J Manage Psychol 23(7):772–788

Seers A (1989) Team-member exchange quality: a new construct for rolemaking research. Organ Behav Hum Decis Process 43(1):118–135

Settoon RP, Bennett N, Liden RC (1996) Social exchange in organizations: perceived organizational support, leader-member exchange, and employee reciprocity. J Appl Psychol 81(3): 219–227

Shamir B (1995) Social distance and charisma: theoretical notes and and exploratory study. Leadersh Q 6(1):19–47

Shamir B (1999) An evaluation of conceptual weaknesses in transformational and charismatic leadership theories. Leadersh Q 10(2):285–306

Shamir B, House RJ, Arthur M (1993) The motivational effects of charismatic leadership. A self-concept based theory. Organ Sci 4(4):577–594

Shaver KG (1985) The attribution of blame. Causality, responsibility, and blameworthiness. Springer, New York

Simpson B, Carroll B (2008) Re-viewing 'role' in processes of identity construction. Organization 15(1):29–50

Skinner BF (1966) Operant behavior. In: Honig W (ed) Operant behavior: areas of research and application. Appleton-Century-Crofts, New York, pp 12–32

Skinner BF (1969) Contingencies of reinforcement. Appleton-Century-Crofts, New York

Sims HP Jr, Lorenzi P (1992) The new leadership paradigm. Social learning and cognition in organizations. Sage, Thousand Oaks, CA

Sims HP, Manz CC (1982) Modeling influences on employee behavior. Pers J 61(1):58–65

Smircich L, Morgan G (1982) Leadership: the management of meaning. J Appl Behav Sci 18(3): 257–273

Sosik JJ, Avolio BJ, Kahai SS (1997) Effects of leadership style and anonymity on group potency and effectiveness in a group decision support system environment. J Appl Psychol 82(1): 89–103

Sparrowe RT (1994) Empowerment in the hospitality industry: an exploration of antecedents and outcomes. Hosp Res J 17(3):51–73

Sparrowe RT, Liden RC (1997) Process and structure in leader-member exchange. Acad Manage Rev 22(2):522–552

Stajkovic AD, Luthans F (1998) Social cognitive theory and self-efficacy: going beyond traditional motivational and behavioral approaches. Organ Dyn 26(4):62–74

Stech EL (1997) Psychodynamic approach. In: Northouse PG (ed) Leadership. Theory and Practice. Sage, Thousand Oaks, CA, pp 184–203

Stech EL (2004) Psychodynamic approach. In: Northouse PG (ed) Leadership. Theory and Practice. Sage, Thousand Oaks, CA, pp 235–264

Stech EL (2006) Psychodynamic approach. In: Northouse PG (ed) Leadership. Theory and practice. Sage, Thousand Oaks, CA, pp 237–264

Stein RT, Heller T (1983) The relationship of participation rates to leadership status: a meta-analysis. In: Blumberg HH, Hare AP, Kent V, Davies MF (eds) Small groups and social interaction. Wiley, Chicester, pp 401–406

Steiner DD (1997) Attributions in leader-member exchanges: implications for practice. Eur J Work Organ Psychol 6(1):59–72

Steyrer J (1998) Charisma and the archetypes of leadership. Organ Stud 19(5):807–828

Stryker S, Statham A (1985) Symbolic interaction and role theory. In: Lindzey G, Aronson E (eds) Handbook of social psychology, vol 1, Theory and method. Lawrence Erlbaum Associates, Hillsdale, NJ, pp 311–378

Stryker S (1980) Symbolic interactionism. Benjamin Cummings, Menlo Park, CA

Tierney WG (1996) Leadership and postmodernism: on voice and the qualitative method. Leadersh Q 7(3):371–384

Tsui AS (1984) A multiple-constituency framework of managerial reputational effectiveness. In: Hunt JG, Hosking D, Schriesheim CA, Steward R (eds) Leaders and managers: International perspectives on managerial behavior and leadership. Pergamon Press, New York, pp 28–44

Turner BA (ed) (1990) Organizational symbolism. Walter de Gruyter, New York

Turner JH (1988) A theory of social interaction. Stanford University Press, Stanford, CA

Van Breukelen W, Schyns B, Le Blanc P (2006) Leader-member exchange theory and research. Accomplishments and future challenges. Leadership 2(3):295–316

Van Seters DA, Field RHG (1990) The evolution of leadership theory. J Organ Change Manage 3(3):29–45

Weber M (1968) Economy and society: an outline of interpretive sociology. Bedminster Press, New York

Weibler J (1995) Symbolische führung [symbolic leadership]. In: Kieser A, Reber G, Wunderer R (eds) Handwörterbuch der Führung. C.E. Poeschel, Stuttgart, pp 2015–2026

Weiner B, Frieze I, Kukla A, Reed L, Rest S, Rosenbaum RM (1987) Perceiving the causes of success and failure. In: Jones EE, Kanouse DE, Kelley HH, Nisbett RE, Valins S, Weiner B (eds) Attribution: perceiving the causes of behavior. Lawrence Erlbaum Associates, Hillsdale, NJ, pp 95–120

Wood RE, Bandura A (1989) Impact of conceptions of ability on self-regulatory mechanisms and complex decision making. J Pers Soc Psychol 56(3):407–415

Wrapp HE (1984) Good managers don't make policy decisions. Harv Bus Rev 62(4):8–21

Yagil D (1998) Charismatic leadership and organizational hierarchy: attribution of charisma to close and distant leaders. Leadersh Q 9(2):161–177

Yukl GA (1994) Leadership in organizations. Prentice Hall, Englewood Cliffs, NJ

Yukl GA (1999) An evaluation of conceptual weaknesses in transformational and charismatic leadership theories. Leadersh Q 10(2):285–305

Yukl GA (2001) Leadership in organizations. Prentice Hall, Englewood Cliffs, NJ

Yukl GA (2006) Leadership in organizations. Prentice Hall, Englewood Cliffs, NJ

Yukl GA, Falbe CM (1990) Influence tactics and objectives in upward, downward, and lateral influence attemps. J Appl Psychol 75(2):132–140

Yukl GA, Falbe CM, Youn JY (1993) Patterns of influence behaviour for managers. Group Organ Manage 18(3):5–28

Yukl GA, Howell JM (1999) Organisational and contextual influences on the emergence and effectiveness of charismatic leadership. Leadersh Q 10(2):257–284

Yukl G, Tracey JB (2002) Consequences of influence tactics used with subordinates, peers, and the boss. J Appl Psychol 77(4):525–535

Zaleznik A (1977) Managers and leaders: are they different? Harv Bus Rev 55:67–68

Index

Breinigsville, PA USA
14 January 2010
230664BV00004B/1/P

9 783790 821574